CLEAR VESSELS

Live a Clear, Joyful, and Guided Life

Sue

Be clear my friend!

Steve

STEVEN JAMES HOFFMAN
CONTRIBUTIONS BY HOLLY BURNS

ISBN: 978-1-7350726-2-3

Wyrd & Wyld Publishing
Spokane, WA 99223

All bible quotations are from the New International Version of The Holy Bible.
THE HOLY BIBLE, NEW INTERNATIONAL VERSION®, NIV® Copyright © 1973, 1978, 1984, 2011 by Biblica, Inc.™ Used by permission. All rights reserved worldwide.

Cover & Layout design: Heather Dakota
www.heatherdakota.com

Author photo by Michelle Richardson
www.michellerichardsonphotography.net

Cover photo: © tutye, Adobe Stock

www.clearvessels.com

This book is dedicated to all the people who are wondering if life is worth living. Don't give up before the magic begins!

CLEAR VESSELS

Live a Clear, Joyful, and Guided Life

The desire to know your own Soul will end all other desires.

~Rumi

CONTENTS

PREFACE

Did you ever ask for a sign—a simple clue, wink, nod, or maybe just a coincidence that would give you hope? Perhaps you didn't even ask for a sign, but nevertheless, one jumped out in front of you? This is a story about one of those days.

Now I get some sort communication every single day. I am not psychic (or are we all psychic?), but I wish I was. Life would be a lot easier with a direct line to the other side. This story goes back to a time when I really needed some hope. Between my desperate state and an unexpected surprise, it made for a rather memorable day. I still count that day as one of my greatest blessings.

It all began on a cold, drizzly, late fall day in western Wisconsin. In retrospect, it started well before that, but don't all of our stories go back further than we care to mention? Anyway, this part of the story started that cold day.

I drove 12 miles to a state park, coincidentally named Hoffman Hills Recreation Area, as in my last name. Synchronicity was already kicking in. This 700-acre preserve consists primarily of tree-covered rolling hills, a few wetlands, and a prairie full of tall, beautiful grasses. With the temp in the low 40s, the drizzle was not far from turning into snow. This weather was perfect for my favorite piece of clothing, a mossy-green Gore-Tex jacket. You know the pullover type with an ample hood that fits well over a stocking cap. This shell, combined fleece under layer, kept me dry and warm as I was hiking up and down the hills. If only we had a similar jacket to protect us from the bumps and bruises of life.

I had relocated to the area a few months earlier, not long after my divorce. Actually, it was my ex-wife's divorce—she was the one who wanted it. I thought moving to a new town might be just what I needed, even though it meant only seeing my two boys every other weekend. The move wasn't what I had hoped for, since I was working about 70 hours per week for a person, at the time, I would have called a narcissistic asshole. Now, I would call him "just another pointer in life." People play the roles that we ask of them. Anger filled me after the divorce, though any change was worth trying. I didn't realize that the pay raise I took with the new job would go straight to my ex-wife in the form of maintenance and child support. Talk about a kick in the shorts— working twice as hard for less money and not being near my boys. Did I mention my boss?

When I wasn't working, I was studying *A Course In Miracles*, a voluminous spiritual course that required a lot of commitment. I was a voracious reader of spiritual books after my divorce. Being raised Catholic, I always had a strong belief in God. One thing puzzled me, though. How could a kid do all the right things in life, end up on his face, and then not have God provide any assistance? You might say I was seeking God, even though I wasn't quite sure what I would say when I found Him.

Perhaps the best thing about hiking in cold, lousy weather is that you won't bump into many people. That day, I had all 700 acres to myself...sort of. I don't know why more people don't hike in the cold. It's a beautiful time of year in the northern states. A stillness covers nature, yet there is a palpable energy.

I think a little moisture in the air makes the energy that much more intense. And the smell of the leaves is something you can't find on a Caribbean island. I got out of my Pathfinder and left it alone in the parking lot. After a short, flat walk, the trail ascended as it meandered into the woods. These words crossed my mind: *Look for the sign.* Was this a thought? Probably. My mind often buzzed like a beehive with its non-stop activity. This was likely just another random thought. I played along, though, hoping it was an important piece of communication. These messages rarely turned out to be anything in the past, but when you're desperate, you cling to anything. I've yelled out for God, angels, Spirit Guides…hell, even a ghost would do: anyone to acknowledge that there is more to all of this thing called life. These efforts produced little in the way of concrete evidence. Maybe it was curiosity, hope, or just nothing else to do, but I decided to follow this particular thought that day. The thought would periodically repeat itself. Funny that I say, "repeat itself." Was *it* repeating itself, or was I?

A while later, I did come to a sign. It was a short, wooden marker about a foot and a half tall that said something like: "this is an oak tree…blah, blah, blah." The kind of sign you expect to see in state parks. Surely, this couldn't be what I was looking for. If so, that would be a pretty lousy joke on the part of the Universe. I wasn't feeling very humorous at this stage of my life.

Progressing down the path, I heard, *Look for the sign,* again. A few more similar park signs appeared, but I began to conclude that I was trying too hard to believe in something that wasn't real. About 15 minutes after giving up on my thoughts, I reached the back peak of the park.

A large observation tower appeared ahead. The oil-treated lumber stretched 60 feet into the sky. At the base was a large sign with bright yellow letters carved into the brown painted planks. Could this be the sign?! My excitement spiked. It was really the last possibility. I began to read the name of the tower in bold print at the top of the sign. Then gradually I moved on to what proved to be nothing more than meaningless information, at least as far as my search was concerned. By the time I was done reading, my hopes had dwindled again. I couldn't believe I fell for another one of these tricks of the mind.

Again, I heard the message, with more vigor than ever, *Look at the sign!* It was then that I noticed a plaque on the ground. One of the contributors to the tower had the last name "Hoffman-Godlove," which I interpreted as "God loves Hoffman." I instantly began to cry. At this moment, I knew that I was not alone. I had never heard of anyone having the last name "Godlove." What were the odds that this was the first time?

I climbed to the top of the tower, wiping away my stream of tears. Once there, I stood slightly shaking, taking in this experience and the incredible view above the canopy of trees. My faith had exploded in size—so much so that I figured I could step off the tower and God would take care of me. Maybe I could even levitate. Worst case, life had been pretty sucky for much of the past 20 years and I would get to go to heaven. I had become tired of the struggle. My better wisdom came over me, though, and I decided I should be thankful for today's gift and begin my journey home.

Since then, a never-ending stream of events has confirmed to me that we are never alone. Not only that, but there is a loving, joyful, humorous, eager presence that is begging to work with us. We have so much potential. The wisdom our Guides share can make life truly magical.

INTRODUCTION

*When setting out on a journey, do not seek advice from
those who have never left home.*

~Rumi

As we stumble through life, we learn many lessons and pick up tools that help us navigate life a little more easily. The wisdom shared with me on my path transformed my life from struggle and depression into one of peace, support, fun, and empowerment. I feel compelled to share these gifts in the hopes that others can benefit as I did.

The direct source of all this information is God, the Universe, Source, Higher Self, collective consciousness, or whatever you want to call it. Use the label that feels most comfortable to you. No matter the label, the Universal laws still apply. You don't even have to believe in God. If you prefer a scientific description of this energy, go with that. To me, the information is way too personal to go with an inanimate description. Personally, I believe in God, but I also think we are extensions of God. God is experiencing Himself/Herself through us. Being made in the image of God, we have access to what I would term Godlike power, sometimes called love. The wisdom provided by this source(s) continues to provide the best life coaching I have ever received. Healing is not a destination, though; it's a lifelong endeavor. As Rumi, the 13th-century poet and mystic, once wrote, and as I have taken as the epigraph of this book, "The desire to know your own Soul will end all other desires."

Holly Burns, a psychic friend whom I met in a quaint, little, Minneapolis bookstore several years ago, taps into this all-knowing source of wisdom through her readings. She calls the voice that speaks to her "the Elders." They did not assign a name to themselves. Holly senses that they are high level "God workers." I suspect they are the all-knowing, collective consciousness that our Souls are a part of. I also think that this "oneness" can be called God. What I do know is that the accuracy, insight, and power of the information they provide blows me away. I was told things that I only said to myself. The Elders intimately knew my feelings, how I approached things, and the best methods to get through my thick skull. While the readings are personal in nature, the lessons apply to all of mankind.

The secondary source of this information is the path that I have followed. My hope is that by hearing my stories, you experience the same hope and joy in your life. We each have our own path, but there are some eternal truths that should benefit us all. I am thankful for the path that I have traveled and will travel. It delights me to share some of that journey with you.

As I was reviewing a printed reading from Holly, the words "this is gold!" jumped out of my mouth. I knew then that I had to share these lessons with the world. Words can be very powerful, as you will learn, so I took note of my exclamation.

The wisdom and truths that cross our paths are reminders of who we really are. If these truths resonate, you are likely in the awakening process. If you find them meaningless, you are merely choosing to experience something different. That does not make any of us better or worse than others. We all arrive home in perfect divine timing.

The world can be challenging with people at various stages

of awakening. It is like there are two entirely different games being played on the same field. As difficult as it can be, resort to compassion when dealing with people who have different beliefs than yours. We may think we have the answers, but each of us has a very limited perspective. We are all on the right path, and we are all playing the role expected of us.

Harnessing the power that is our birthright is a process that requires discipline and the breaking old habits. We are on a journey to become aware of the love that is available to us and more importantly, aware of the love that we are. Finally, don't think of this process as work. It is supposed to be fun!

SECTION ONE
Clearing

In this first section, we set the foundation for our self-discovery. This is where we clear the doubts, fears, and beliefs that are limiting the flow of abundance. This section is based primarily on my life experiences and the key influences that have assisted me along the way. Following these simple exercises may change your life. They certainly changed mine.

To use a gardening analogy, this is the part where the soil is prepped. If you are in a dark or unhappy place, more time may be required, and that's okay. You will become aware of and heal low-vibrating energies that block the flow of life. Several tools will be provided. Utilize the ones that work for you and discard the rest. Know you are on the right path, and everything you need will be provided.

CLEAR VESSELS

I am a hole in a flute through which God's breath flows. Listen to the Music!
~Hafiz

Becoming a clear, receptive vessel through which the creative force flows is the most powerful work we can do in our lives.

Pause and read that sentence again. Let it soak into your memory. I have nothing more profound to share than that one sentence. Everything else in this book will point toward that goal.

What does it mean to be clear? It is a state that is absent of fears, doubts, ego, or any other blockages that limit the flow of the Universe, or the communication with God and our Spirit Guides. It is a perfect state of allowing, listening, and observing: it is a state of spaciousness. It is in this spaciousness that miracles manifest. Clarity also awakens us to the miracles that are already around us. Simply staring at a blade of grass can open up a sense of reverence, as every little thing is a microcosm of the Universe's unimaginable splendor.

I love this Hafiz quote because it provides a mental framework for our conscious work, or more accurately, conscious play. By viewing ourselves as the "hole in the flute," we can scan for blockages that restrict the flow. We can scan our thoughts, our minds, and our bodies with an accepting awareness that will help clear and heal these blockages, which often include stories of our past with which we identify. It has been said that our stories are excuses for why we are not happy now. But are you aware of the stories you are telling yourself?

The quote also takes a great burden off us by letting us know what our role is in the creative process. We do not have to push the air through the flute. We do not have to be the fingers that cover the holes in perfect rhythm. The only thing we have to do is surrender our old ways and allow. Non-resistance is the key to the clearing phase.

Knowing that we don't have to *do* anything creates a stillness in our minds that eliminates many blockages from arising. All we really have to do is *be.* When we think of goals or tasks to perform, our minds often begin to think of obstacles. However, our minds are relying on their limited capacity and past experiences. This dampens any enthusiasm that encompassed the original idea.

Being in a state of clarity allows inspired thoughts and aligned actions to take place. It allows us to tap into the wisdom that is far greater than the knowledge of our human minds. We can relax into knowing that all actions and steps necessary to bring the idea to completion will come to us at the right time. Acting without first finding clarity results in struggle and effort. We must develop this new way of creating. This new way involves trust, surrender, self-awareness, and going with the flow. "Going with the flow" is an often-used saying, but it took many life experiences for me to find its true meaning.

I admire many successful visionaries who are engrossed with their end goal that they don't bother to think of why something won't work. They *know* it will.

The first step in becoming a clear vessel involves removing blockages, or as I call it, weeding the garden of our Soul. There are some huge weeds to remove: the biggest for many of us is the lack of self-love. Many smaller ones show up as vibrations in our thoughts or physical body. With practice, we become adept at pulling the big weeds, and plucking the roots of small ones.

The Universe is saying, "Allow me to flow through you unrestricted and you will see the greatest magic you have ever seen."

~Klaus Joehle

After some initial weeding, we discover ways to fertilize the soil, introduce new plants and allow our gardens to blossom in ways too beautiful to fully predict. Eventually, the flowers are so thick that there is no room for weeds. We begin to enjoy the beauty, aroma, and the miracle that each flower represents—the beauty that the ensemble comes together to create, and the intricate patterns of the leaves, petals, and roots, so complex that no group of engineers could have possibly designed them.

This process will become the most exciting and rewarding venture we have ever undertaken. It will become a lifelong endeavor that will allow our passions and self-expression to flourish. It will take us places we had always hoped to go and to places we never imagined. This garden is symbolic of how beautiful our lives can become. By the end of this book, you will be on your way to becoming the gardener of your Soul.

Our ongoing practice will become a balancing act between enjoying the current beauty in and around us and creating future images through an explosion of new and exciting thoughts. We cannot become clear and not have creative ideas flow through us. The positive momentum is inevitable. As we bask in the glow of these positive thoughts and feelings, we start calling forth images from the invisible plane to be manifested into our reality.

Once we notice the connection between our thoughts and the manifestations that arise, we come to realize the incredible power that we possess. We will dance with the Universe. We become magicians of sorts, masters of allowing.

Jesus answered them, "Is it not written in your law,
"I have said you are 'gods?'"

~John 10:34

Having a toolbox of be-happy tricks allows us to easily and quickly access the state of allowing in any situation. Spending 15 minutes in this state at the start of each day will be more productive than the rest of the day spent in physical or mental labor. It will also make the actions we take that much more productive.

As we progress in our practice, keep an air of this heightened awareness throughout the day, or at least remind ourselves of it periodically. Going about your day, carry a smile on your face as if you have a secret that no one else knows. Others will know something is up and will respond differently to you, as will the Universe.

Functioning in a state of clarity is a form of multi-tasking. On one hand, we pay attention to the external world. We need to drive our cars, go to work, shop for groceries, etc. While we are doing those tasks, we are somewhat detached—as Jesus said, "Be passersby." The tasks we perform are not that meaningful. We are the awareness, or the space, in which all things happen. This silent spaciousness is the womb of creation and will reveal the true nature of who you really are.

Clarity is where the magic happens. This may sound like an exaggeration, and as you progress through this book and begin practicing the methods, you will realize that it is not an exaggeration. Miracles are everyday occurrences.

Use the affirmations and meditations in this book, or create your own. Find other affirmations and meditations that resonate to help you manage your own vibrations.

Meditation

Before we get into our first meditation, here are a few quick pointers. My primary goal when meditating is to disengage the mind from its normal stream of rambling thoughts. This allows me to sink into a relaxing place of stillness. I find it difficult to stop thinking completely. To help with this, my meditations give my mind a small task to make it think it is being useful. I call this "giving the dog a bone." As long as the dog has a bone, it won't be barking incessantly. Have you ever noticed how relaxed you become when driving on a long, straight road? Your mind has just enough to focus on for the quiet, subconscious part of you to emerge. To begin each meditation, I prefer to sit upright in a comfortable position and take a couple of deep breaths. I pretend my body is a balloon, and that each inhale stretches me slightly. Then, I feel the relaxing contraction on the exhale. With that in mind, here is our first meditation:

Imagine your body's inner shape being lined with a layer of shiny, titanium metal.

As you mentally observe this lining from the inside, notice that it is shaped exactly as you desire your body to be. Perhaps you have six-pack abs, or nicely toned muscles—whatever you want your body to look like. Maybe you are perfectly happy with the current shape.

Viewing from the inside of the shell, scan your empty vessel for negative thoughts, beliefs, or other blockages that show up as black chunks sticking to the sides. These black chunks look similar to coal. You might find some in the head area, or maybe in the stomach. Ask your Spirit Guides to help by pointing out subtle or hidden black chunks.

Mentally chip away any black chunks with a chisel. Allow the debris to be sucked away by a beautiful golden tube that runs from the small of your back into the center of the Earth, where it all melts away.

Once all the big chunks are gone, go in and buff away any remnants of these blockages with a magic cloth. Notice how clean and shiny the surface has become. You are a clear vessel.

Now, power wash the inside of your vessel. Warm, soapy water comes rushing in through the top of your head. This water has a unique acid in it that makes your titanium shell sparkle brilliantly. The water rushes down to your feet and back up to your head. It looks like a car wash with all the bubbly water splashing everywhere. When everything is clean, allow the water to drain out the same golden tube at your lower spine.

To prevent future blockages, liquid gold pours into your body, again from the top of your head. It flows down and fills up your feet and rises into your legs. Feel a warm energy as it tingles up your body. The gold continues filling your hips, chest, back, and into your arms, and up through your neck and head. As the gold spills out the top of your scalp, it forms a glittery, white cloud that surrounds the outside of your body. Now, you are a clear, golden, sparkling entity.

But it gets better! There is a beautifully jeweled cord that runs from the middle of your back up to the Universe. Plug this into the all-knowing, all-loving Universe. When you do, see your titanium-lined, gold-filled body illuminate with a bright, green glow—or any color you prefer.

Now imagine breathing in and out through your heart, the radiant glow around you expands. Eventually, your rays of light expand endlessly into the Universe. Being plugged into the Universe, your luminous presence now acts like a giant magnet that attracts nothing but abundance and love. Take a minute to enjoy the expansive, golden, electric, loving feeling.

Say to yourself: I am that encompassing. I am that magnificent. I am that amazing. I am that powerful.

Affirmations

A quick note on using affirmations: The key is to find ones that resonate with you. Find one that taps into the feelings you desire. Then, soak it in for as long as you can. Repeat several, or just focus on one. Go with what feels right. Keep a list and refer to them frequently. There are many sources to follow that send a steady stream of affirmations your way. Personally, I find social media apps such as Tumblr, Pinterest, and Facebook very helpful. Take a screenshot with your cell phone of your favorite quotes. This provides a gallery that you can visit frequently when you have a few idle moments. Affirmations assist in raising your vibration quickly. Basking in a high vibration feeling is a form of meditation in itself. The affirmations on the next page reinforce the process of becoming a clear vessel.

I am clear. I am free. I am powerful. I am love. I am purpose. I am joy.
What if I became so clear that I allowed the Universe
to deliver unrestricted good today?
I am a clear vessel through which the Universe flows.
I am clear and confident in every facet of my life.
My thoughts are becoming clearer, stronger, and more positive every day.
I am so much clearer than I was yesterday.
My level of clarity becomes greater and greater every day.
This is the clearest I have ever been.
I love knowing that the clearer I get, the better my life becomes.
My nature is clarity.
I am a master allower and a master manifester.
I create space for miracles to happen.
Five minutes of pure thought will change my life.
How much will I allow, at what pace, and from where?

EGO

Surrender yourself humbly, then you can be trusted to care for all things.

~Lao Tzu*

Ego is likely the most documented topic in the history of psychology. The descriptions, definitions, and analyses of ego are seemingly endless.

I view the ego as an entity created by an overly active mind. This entity is based entirely on our individual perspectives of the world. This confined perspective creates the belief that we our separate from the whole. Being separate, the ego seeks to defend and promote itself. This is the grand illusion of life. Walking on planet Earth requires a certain degree of self-preservation, and in the process, we seem to forget the oneness from which we came. The busyness of our minds masks the oneness that is accessible in stillness.

When the mind feasts, Reality disappears;
when the mind fasts, Reality enters.

~Nisargadatta Maharaj

Philosophically, I believe we are each a perspective of the same whole. In other words, God created us so He/She can experience Himself/Herself from different vantage points. We are individuations of God, made in His/Her image, but the reality is, we are all one. The well-known quote from Rumi touches on a common metaphor used to describe the relationship between individuals and the oneness of God.

You are not a drop in the ocean. You are the entire ocean in a drop.

~Rumi*

The ego can become problematic when the separation instead of unity, becomes the focus. In 2016, author and marketer, Ryan Holiday wrote an international bestselling book, *Ego is the Enemy*. The book highlights several examples of successful people whose demise was brought on by their excessive ego.

In my opinion, a lengthy discussion is not necessary. There is a shortcut.

The greatest benefit of becoming a clear vessel, other than living an empowered life, is the knowledge that we are vehicles for God to work through; thus, all glory and honor belong to God. We are much like a fire hose, and God is the water. We are an instrument for directing God's power (or Universal energy, if you prefer). Because of this, we stand in gratitude and reverence of this power, knowing that we are not its original source. We are grateful that we were the chosen channel for this flow. This knowledge prevents the downfalls that Ryan Holiday describes.

By myself I can do nothing.

~John 5:30

Also, many of Holiday's examples are not successful if success is measured by the amount of joy in our lives. His subjects were deemed successful due to outwardly apparent gains in wealth, power, or fame. If we seek validation in the external world, however, we will fail. We may achieve wealth, power, and fame, but these alone cannot produce true happiness. If we build our houses in this sand, they will eventually crumble.

Attaining success by becoming a clear vessel for God and by following our bliss may result in external rewards, but that is not the goal. The goal is to lead a joy-filled life by allowing God's energy to flow through us unrestricted. By the way, external manifestations will be a likely by-product of the flow. Get happy and everything else follows. The flow is the goal. These types of gains are lasting. When your body is gone, your Soul will retain this growth.

Meditation

Begin by breathing directly into your heart.

The energy from this breath expands throughout your body.

*As your body radiates, lose track of your physical form
and become a glowing ball of light.*

Now, begin to move toward the sun.

*As you get closer, the temperature gets hotter and hotter, but because you are a
ball of light it does not affect you. Think to yourself:
I am indestructible and everlasting.*

*Allow attachments, beliefs, hurts, and memories
that do not serve you to burn away.
The roles you play in life also burn away.*

*Say to yourself:
I am no longer identified by my profession, past failures
or accomplishments, or even familial roles.*

These are all temporary roles that I am playing in this lifetime.

All that is left is who I really am.

I am conscious energy. I am a powerful creative force.

I am now. I am free. I am joy.

I am.

SELF-LOVE

You yourself, as much as anybody in the entire Universe,
deserve your love and affection.

~Buddha*

The biggest obstacle to clarity, for many, is a lack of self-love.

If parents could help their children continue to love themselves as much as they do at birth, most of the world's problems would disappear. You can only give what you are filled up with. If you hate yourself, you will give hate to the world. If you love yourself, you will emanate an endless supply of love.

Somehow, after birth, our perspective of ourselves dwindles. We grow up trying to please friends, parents, teachers, employers, society, etc. There are specific standards that we must pass to be considered worthy. We need to attain good grades, work enough hours, dress and speak in the proper manner, meet the sales goals…it is a never-ending pursuit.

When we don't conform to these standards, we are often made aware of our failures. Eventually, no one needs to tell us that we are a failure. The message has sunk in enough that we start to beat ourselves up and begin to believe it in our heart.

Trying to measure up to the outside world is where the mistake originates.

Even if we meet all the world's standards, we still lose because we are looking for happiness in the wrong place. We can search the outside world for an eternity and not find real and lasting happiness. It must be found within. As Jesus said, "The Kingdom of God is within you!"

Lack of self-love can be very complicated, with many sources and layers. Much practice and patience may be required to heal. It could take a lifetime. Self-love is such an essential part of the process that we need to discuss it. I hope that many of you have already attained a certain level of self-love, so that we can focus more on fine-tuning our energetic vibrations. For those who are not quite there, I hope my stories let you know that you are not alone and there is hope. Look for an opening to occur that begins your own transformation. The process is about forgetting the image the ego has created so you can see how creative, powerful, and lovable you really are.

To accomplish this, we must take responsibility for our own inner clarity and vibration. Not enough people understand how to do this. We are playing a game where we do not know the rules. It's like thinking we are playing checkers when it is a game of chess. We have good intentions, but then don't understand why most of our moves end in frustration.

I intend to share the real "rules" of this game of life—rules that I discovered through trial and error. Life can be joyful, fun, and miraculous when we are playing by the right rules. We have access to fantastic power; we just need to learn how to access it. Best of all, it's quite easy, much easier than struggling through life as I did for my first 40 years.

As you read my personal stories, become aware of your stories. We all have stories, and we all have pains. It's up to us to realize that our stories are not who we are. They are reflections of what you are thinking, how you are feeling, and, quite possibly, guideposts directing you to who you really are.

You are the greatest project you will ever work on.
Take your time. Create Magic.

~*Unknown*

My search for self-love began with what I call my river story.

River Story

Late one night during my divorce, I first yelled out to God, "Just tell me what the rules are!" I had been a faithful servant yet ended up losing. Little in life was working out well. It was a depressing struggle, although superficially many would have viewed me as being successful with a pretty good life. My life's mission was to live up to what I perceived to be the expectations of the outside world, and I was pretty good at that. But that is not the game we are supposed to be playing.

> *Create a life that feels good on the inside,*
> *not one that just looks good on the outside.*
>
> *~Unknown*

That night I asked for a sign that I was not alone, and I got nothing. Feeling despondent, I descended a steep hill to the river bottom behind my house. It didn't matter that this was late winter with at least a couple feet of snow on the ground. I wandered out to a narrow point of land that stuck out into the river. Picnic Point, as I called it, included remnants of an old lumber mill that existed a hundred years prior. The point was a mesmerizing place to reflect. On the upstream side was a large, swirling pool where the logs would gather. Downstream consisted of shallow, choppy rapids. Being winter, the river was frozen except for patches where the rapids proved too fast to freeze.

During a previous spring flood, an enormous stump had washed up on this point. The stump provided protection from the blowing snow and created a deep snowdrift that served as the perfect seat. With the river a few feet away, I weighed the pros and cons of suicide, not knowing how serious I was. It was partially an analytical assessment, but it was no doubt highly emotional, too. Two friends had committed suicide under similar, divorce-related circumstances earlier in my life. I could fully relate to their struggles. I still think of them frequently and like to believe that they have helped me on my journey.

I did not get answers that night, but I did not give up either. Life did begin to change. The search for myself began, though I was not fully aware of it at the time.

A few months later, I moved away to the town I spoke of in the preface to this book. While the story of finding the sign of "Hoffman-Godlove" was huge to me, it was not my first encounter with messages coming to me. Beginning on the night of the river visit, a recurring thought that said *We need you* started to appear in my mind, but I dismissed it until the following event happened.

As part of my divorce therapy, I had purchased a motorcycle and was out riding one day. Thoughts seemed to blow right off me during peaceful country rides. During a pocket of clarity on this ride, a song I had not heard before appeared in my head. The lyrics were all about "now." Soon after, a bookstore appeared on the right side of the road. I could not resist stopping in to see if anything grabbed me. I went in and started walking down an aisle until it came to a "T." Standing there, my next thought was not to turn right or left. My eyes froze, staring forward as I saw several rows filled with *The Power of Now* by Eckhart Tolle. I may be thick-headed at times, but it was apparent that I was supposed to read this book. I'm not sure which impacted me more—knowing that I was directed to this book, or the book itself. To this day, I am amused at how the books or people we need in our lives always arrive at just the right time.

Whenever anyone is in a state where even the slightest contemplation of suicide is present, it should be very apparent that self-love is lacking. One-by-one, books, signs, and messages gradually pulled me out of the depths.

Another book that really improved my perspective on life was *Your Soul's Plan* by Robert Schwartz. In it, Schwartz analyzes several life stories through the lens of psychics with varying talents. I gained two things from his book. First, no matter how messed up someone's life may appear, there is a reason and a divine plan behind it. This reminds us to have compassion for everyone (especially ourselves) and restrain from judging others. We don't even fully understand our own stories, so who are we to judge others?

My second takeaway is that I connected with Staci Wells, one of the psychics who assisted with Schwartz's book. Staci performs past-life and pre-birth planning readings as a part of her services. These readings provide a blueprint of some of the significant goals and obstacles one planned for their current lifetime.

I received many lessons in these readings. My hope is that they help you see that there is a rhyme and reason to your life.

Here are the lessons that Staci shared with me during my pre-birth planning reading. These are my interpretations, so it is possible that I did not get everything exactly right from Staci.

Staci Wells – Reading

1) Self-Perfection – Souls seeking this goal have come a long way and want to attain a level of mastery. It can be a toughy! It's about perfecting ourselves, not others. But it can make us idealistic and impatient with others. We must learn to focus on ourselves, not others, which requires plenty of internal work and alone time. Much energy is created, which can affect our nervous systems if not properly managed through exercise and meditation. The paradox of this lesson is that to perfect ourselves, we must provide tools for others.
A high level of compassion for others is also part of this lesson.

2) Balance – This is the second most challenging lesson behind self-perfection, and it can affect all areas of our lives. For example, emotional extremes could result in swings in financial affairs. The goal is to find an emotional center-point and maintain that connection throughout life. If we feel good about ourselves, our monetary needs will take of themselves. If this lesson is not handled well, more extreme issues such as bipolar disorder or schizophrenia may appear in order to steer us in the right direction. As you can see, even things that seem "bad" are good. Best of all, we are destined to succeed.

3) Emotional Independence – This lesson asks us to learn that we are the source of our happiness and well-being. Soul agreements with others may be involved. In my case, I had planned to have my marriage end. Staci says that in a previous lifetime, I was courting my ex-wife from this lifetime. I found her with a lover and killed him in a fit of rage. My divorce provided an opportunity to handle this challenge better. Staci says I passed with flying colors. I don't know that I would have graded myself that highly based on the anger I experienced. We get multiple opportunities to pass these lessons. We might as well pass these tests as quickly as possible and enjoy life. Another observation on all these lessons is that we need to be patient with ourselves.
The person I killed, by the way, is now my youngest son.
I gave him new life as part of my karmic duty.

4) Compassion – Souls with this goal seek to attain higher levels of compassion and to be of service to others. This may require more responsibility to family (family members often serve as our teachers and testers), but we must learn that family also includes all of mankind. We need to detach from anger and blame and have no expectations of others or situations. The goal is to shift from anger to compassion at a high level. Then, we can be of service to the masses.

5) Spiritual Growth of Self – Through enrichment of relationship with ourselves, we can connect with self, Soul, and all that is. Attainment of these great rewards, however, requires self-assessment, patience, compassion for self and more alone time than most others take on. It can be confrontational. Too much money can be a distraction. If we don't pass this lesson, we could veer way off course and become out-of-balance in future lifetimes.

6) Self-Esteem, Self-Worth, and Self-Expression – This asks us to learn our truths and live life at a high level of self-expression of those truths. Find what brings us alive and gives us energy. Find our truths and express them! I challenged myself to bring forth knowledge. Soul agreements with my family called for a "less than nurturing" environment, which would send me looking within. Note to my family: I thought I had a good childhood—definitely better than most! No regrets here, but I hope you are not offended by Staci's "less than nurturing" comment, as I felt, and still feel, fortunate for all of you being in my life.

The above lessons were designed to teach self-empowerment and allow for greater self-expression, to the ultimate benefit of everyone. All the good we send out comes back threefold. Before we can give, however, we must gain clarity and fill ourselves with love. Only then can we provide service and value to others.

Another benefit from this exercise is the knowledge that we are brave souls for leaving the comfort of heaven to come down and deal with challenges and unpleasant situations in an effort to bring beauty and love to all. We are never alone in this endeavor. We created intricate plans and are supported by a staff of Spirit Guides who are constantly by our side. These Guides see us as the perfect beings that we are and love to help as much as we will allow them.

Whole by Brian Seth Hurst was another book that found its way to me. For those who are struggling with self-love, this may be an excellent place to start. Brian is a sincere, multi-talented person who, among other things, is an intuitive reader and life coach.

As I was reading his book, the statement "I am enough" almost alarmed me. I had never even contemplated that thought; instead, I was always trying to improve myself, or maybe more so, trying to prove myself. This was a huge revelation. The full quote from Brian's book is, "When the belief at work is 'I am enough,' you create a world in which you need not satisfy a list of conditions in order to be loved."

By the time I was done reading *Whole*, I had revised the affirmation from "I am enough" to "I am more than enough; I am pretty frickin' awesome."

Discovering and truly knowing self-love is not a one-time event. Fully healing is a process of peeling back layers. Sometimes you think you have moved past an old wound and it pops up again. Don't be discouraged. Acknowledge it, observe it, and wrap your loving awareness around it. Know that you are always doing your best given your perspective and awareness at any given time. Also, these hurts were not meaningless; they were directing you to somewhere better. I will address this healing process in more detail in the next chapter.

Before ending this chapter, I want to expand one last time on just how important self-love is. Referring to Hafiz' quote, *"I am a hole in a flute through which God's breath flows. Listen to the Music!,"* lacking self–love would be equivalent to putting a big wad of chewing gum in the hole of the flute. Life simply won't work without it. Everything depends on your concept of yourself. When you realize that you are the source of love, you will no longer have to search for it. You will tap into an endless supply, not only for you, but for others.

Self-love is needed for the creation process that we cover in Section Two of this book. Creating, which can be more accurately described as allowing, mostly depends on loving ourselves and being open, but not attached, to whatever comes our way.

Affirmations

I bring the highest value by being myself.

I am making a difference in a fun, easy, joyful way.

I am fully supported in all of my affairs.

My energetic path is of immeasurable value to the Universe.

My passions easily create my happiness and abundance.

I am creating a life in which my ideas are valued and respected.

My life will become as good as I allow it to be.

I am open to it being better than I imagined.

Life is much easier than I thought possible.

I am calm and collected and open to receive the abundance of the Universe.

Nothing in nature blooms all year long, including me.

Being of the world, it is only natural for me to ebb and flow.

I am allowed to be perfect and growing all at the same time.

I am loved. I am supported. I can do no wrong.

I've done better than I know. I've helped more than I realize.

And I'm closer than I think.

I am more than enough.

HEALING OURSELVES

You always have the power to make yourself feel better.

~The Elders

Let's face it—life can be tough. We've all had more than our share of stuff thrown at us. There have been disappointments, broken hearts, and dashed dreams. We've been repressed, and at times, got worse than we deserved. We've had so many emotional kicks to the gut that we sometimes wonder if it is all worthwhile. And frankly, the ending doesn't always make sense. Sometimes Soul Agreements require personal sacrifice to implement change for the good of the whole. High-level Souls often take on tough challenges. I'm sure these individuals don't always remember these agreements as they encounter earthly struggles.

The only thing I'm aware of that can help with extreme situations is faith. We just don't fully understand God's plans sometimes.

With smaller challenges, we can heal ourselves. Pain and sorrow block the flow of life. Healing ourselves opens the flow and allows us to navigate life more gracefully and enjoyably.

I want to address two specific areas for healing: restrictive beliefs and emotional pain. Until we heal these beliefs and wounds, negative patterns persist. It has been said that when certain people and situations no longer serve us, they leave us. We will keep getting the same tests in different forms until we pass them, and in some cases, until we become experts in dealing with them. In these cases, revisiting past hurts and beliefs can be productive for clearing fertile ground for new growth.

Our end goal is to live in the present and manage the vibration we are currently sending out to the world. The power is in this moment. Because of this, avoid dwelling too much on the past. The past was a different lifetime and now has limited use. Even current external conditions can largely be ignored because they are the result of past thoughts and feelings. That's why we need to steer our life by managing our current vibrations with little regard for external circumstances. Reacting to current external events is like driving your car while looking out the back window.

When the same troublesome pattern persists, however, it is time to take notice. This requires a high level of self-awareness, or perhaps someone else to point it out. Typically, these patterns are tied to beliefs we learned in childhood. Finding the root belief can be beneficial, but it is not necessary. Merely being aware of a non-productive belief will start to dissolve its effect. For example, perhaps you have unrealistic fears about catching a disease. Even if you do not know the source of the fear, observing this fear and replacing it with more positive beliefs can help.

Remember, a belief is just a thought we repeat enough to become our personal truth. A habit of negative thoughts creates a negative belief. How is this belief serving us? Do we want to replace it with something better? If so, changing our thought patterns can change our beliefs, and thus change our lives.

Healing Restrictive Beliefs

Let me provide a couple of short, personal examples of restrictive beliefs, and how we might correct them.

The first one involves my dad. There was a vast ranch going up for auction near our small town in South Dakota. It was expected to sell for tens of millions of dollars. I commented that it seemed like a risky proposition to auction the property. "How many people could possibly show up to bid on a property of that size?" I asked. Dad convincingly responded, "Oh, there's a lot of money out there."

Dad worked his tail off his entire life. I thought that was the secret to his success. Through several of his own successful ventures and comments like the one above, I soon realized that his mental game was also a critical component. He's like a cat —he always lands on his feet. He has great faith in that ability, and great faith in God. He has a trust, or sense of knowing, that everything will turn out right. More recently, dad was diagnosed with cancer and given 6 to 24 months to live. He told us, "It's not like I'm dying or anything!" About nine months into his battle, he was declared cancer free.

My brothers seemed to pick up on Dad's financial traits better than I did. I'm the one who went to college for business, was considered the "smart one" in the family, and had a professional investment career, yet the other three all exceeded my financial success.

When my youngest brother graduated from college, he set out to start a home-building business. He needed a $40,000 loan to buy the basic equipment. I didn't want to diminish his confidence, but I thought that there was no way a bank would give money to some kid fresh out of college. I should know: I was a loan officer at one time. Well, he got the loan and became the homebuilder of the year in a relatively large market. He followed that up with many other successful pursuits.

You see, my family members just assumed they would succeed. It's as if they would assuredly ask, "Why wouldn't it work?" Meanwhile, I was always coming up with what could go wrong. Do you see the vibrational difference in our thinking, and more importantly, our feelings?

To achieve greater financial success, I had to realize the story I was telling and change it. To what stories do you beat the drum? Look at your current circumstances for your first clues.

Replacing the limiting belief, rather than just trying to drop the old view, can be extremely helpful. Instead of thinking about a lack of money, focus on things that are working. Changing the direction of our focus will change our entire world. I call this having a single-eyed view. We are either looking at what's working, or we are looking at what's not. Choose wisely.

Choose for yourselves this day whom you will serve.
~Joshua 24:15

Repeating daily affirmations of wealth is another possible solution. One alternative to the usual positive affirmations is to phrase them in the form of questions. For example, perhaps meditating on this statement will help: "What if today I allowed the Universe to provide in unrestricted ways?" The Universe loves questions. Test the Universe. There is infinite wisdom available to you once you learn to tap into it.

Questions sometimes work more effectively than statements on our minds. They take us out of a place of knowing and open us up to much greater wisdom. It is also a softer way to change our mood. If you repeat the affirmation "I am rich," but don't believe it, the words feel forced and do not have the intended effect. It might actually make you feel worse. Instead, an affirmation like, "What if I allowed the Universe to provide abundance in perfect ways and at the perfect time?" may find a back door into your psyche. Statements like these may awaken you to opportunities that you were not seeing before. If the opportunities feel good, take inspired action.

Healing Emotional Hurts

Do any of us escape this life without at least one romantic heartbreak? These events genuinely feel like a dagger to our hearts. This is because emotional wounds result in physical symptoms. I am not going to list all possible sources of emotional pain; I'll just speak from where I have the most experience—the ending of a relationship.

This is one of those lessons that I have much experience with. I already discussed my past-life experience where I killed someone when I caught him with the lady of my affection. In this lifetime, an early adulthood breakup left me reeling for years. Next, there was the end of a ten-year marriage that sent me on my spiritual path, and then an even longer relationship ended after that… among others. Damn, that sucks!

Here is a quick little healing technique that I learned that can help lessen the pain. This technique can work for any pain, but especially emotional pains. Here's how it goes:

Find a pleasant spot in nature and sit on the ground. Under the protection of a friendly tree might be a good choice. Imagine yourself inhaling energy up from the Earth into the base of your spine, through your torso, and past your head. As you exhale, let the energy reverse back down your spine and into the Earth. Let this energy flush through your seven chakras (seven energy centers that run from the root of your spine to just above your head).

As you continue to breathe in this manner, your mind begins to quiet.

When going through a relationship breakup, our minds can run out of control. Giving the mind something to focus on—like this breathing exercise—allows it to disengage from the endless icky thoughts.

Emotional pain lodges in the body, typically in the heart or a lower chakra such as the solar plexus or navel area.

Use your awareness to inquire about the pain. What does heartache feel like in your body? Where does it reside? Maybe you feel a pit in your stomach, or perhaps it is in the heart area.

Observe this physical pain. Now imagine that you are breathing directly into and out of the area that hurts. Spend some time with this. Observing the pain without doing anything about it, detaches you from it. The hurt is something in your body; it is not you. Welcome it and ask it to reveal itself.

You may want to go back to the original breathing technique on P21, flushing energy up and down your spine. This can wash away some of the physical pain and get the energy flowing in your body again. Allow the pain to wash into the healing center of the Earth.

Repeat this process as often as needed. After a few days, the pain will be less severe. Just keep peeling back the layers of hurt until it is no longer necessary.

Pain, emotional or physical, is a common stimulant for growth, but it is not the only one. As we become adept at monitoring and managing our energetic vibrations, hopefully we won't need discomfort to steer us in the right direction. We will be ahead of the curve, bringing solutions before the problems appear. To use our gardening metaphor, we will be eradicating weeds before they show on the surface.

Visualization

I want to add a quick comparison between visualizations and meditations. Meditations are designed to quiet the mind and bring stillness. This stillness opens us to the wisdom of the Universe. Visualizations use our imaginations, and thus our minds, to create desired feelings through pictures. The Universe will answer your feeling with something that is a match. I view mediations as an allowing exercise and visualizations as a creating exercise.

During my growth process, the Universe provided a comforting visualization that reminded me to not take life too seriously and go at a pace that feels comfortable. After all, the overall goal is to enjoy the journey.

Here is that reminder:

*At the first stoplight on my way to work, my car faces a radio tower that stretches thousands of feet high. This is my daily reminder to climb one rung higher today: to feel just one rung better. That's easy to do, and it feels good. Some days, however, my morning practice has me feeling so good by the time I leave for work that I just picture myself at the top of the tower. I sit there in bliss, enjoying the view and attracting all the things that are important to me. I see myself sending out the frequency of abundance to the Universe.
I can do this because I am abundant.*

Other days, the top of the tower is hidden by clouds or fog. Just because I can't see the top does not mean that it is not there. This is the same trust that we need to apply to our growth process. You may not see the immediate benefits, but one day you will wake thinking this is the happiest you have ever been. Soon, you will be stringing together several weeks in a row where you are in this state.

The fog is also symbolic of the things we have created on the spiritual or invisible plane. Just because we can't see them does not mean they are not there. The way to attain them is to feel one rung better today. Small changes in our consciousness can have enormous effects. Don't think that the task at hand is too large or too hard. The best part to me is that our vibrations can only go higher. We cannot fall back down. Sure, there may be off days, but our base frequency continues to get better and better with every day that we decide to climb a rung on the ladder. If we can make ourselves feel one rung better, we have the power to do anything. This is very attainable.

CONVERSING WITH OTHERS

Nothing in the world can bother you as much as your own mind, I tell you.
In fact, others seem to be bothering you, but it is not others.
It is your own mind.

~Sri Sri Ravi Shankar*

The gains we make by increasing self-love, keeping the ego at bay, healing our wounds, and revisiting old beliefs will eventually bring us to a higher level of consciousness.

The world will generally seem more cooperative. We will be going with the flow more often, have an improved self-awareness, and feel a greater sense of empowerment.

Then, it will happen. Someone else will burst our bubble of tranquility with words or actions that set us off. Triggers like this are begging for our attention. This is an excellent time to sit back and say, "Well, would you look at that. Apparently, I have some internal work to do." Having internal work to do is alright. It happens to all of us. We want to get to the point where our self-empowerment is not conditioned upon who or what is around.

Personally, I have tried to avoid conflict most of my life. Staying at the surface level of conversations or relationships has been my favorite tactic. This allowed for self-protection and also served as a form of respect to others, or so I told myself. Who wants to be poked? Rather than ask questions, I would make assumptions from high-level observations. If I didn't like what I saw, I would walk away or keep that person at a distance.

Avoiding difficult situations is not the answer. This approach causes the world to close in on us, and we become smaller. We want to open up to an expansive world, to be free to go wherever we want, and be comfortable in any environment.

This is where we leverage the lessons in self-love and awareness. Just as we observe ourselves in a non-judgmental space, we now do the same with others.

One simple but extremely powerful communication tool is asking questions. Forcing ourselves to ask at least two inquisitive or clarifying questions to others can result in greater understanding, trust, and openness. It will deepen relationships and open the path for more joy to flow into our lives.

Working with financial clients, I witnessed these benefits firsthand. One particular time, I was visiting with a client for a routine financial review. Her portfolio was performing well, and there was plenty of money to fund her retirement. All was good.

The client then stated half-jokingly, "I should be spending more money." Rather than laugh this off as small talk, I decided to inquire about this peculiar statement.

"Are you not doing or buying something that you would like to?" I inquired.

"No," she responded. "I have a nice house, take vacations, have a relatively new car; there is nothing else that I want or need."

Becoming more puzzled, I said, "I don't understand. If you have everything you want, why should you be spending more money?"

"Well," she said introspectively, "it's just that my parents ran out of money, and I have a fear that the same thing could happen to me."

Hiding under her original comment were emotions that her financial advisor should know. Knowing her root concerns, I was now better equipped to address the situation.

I left the meeting shortly after, leaving my client and coworker to wrap up some remaining agenda items. After the meeting had adjourned, my coworker came to me for our post-meeting debrief. The client had told him that she had never felt so understood by an advisor. These gains were made possible because I asked two follow-up questions to a comment. This conversation increased trust, understanding, and openness that not only enhanced the relationship in the current moment, but also allowed it to grow more going forward. When you connect with clients at that level, they don't leave. The same connection can be made in personal relationships, too.

What makes this level of connection possible? It is the courage and confidence that comes not from ego-based thoughts, but from feelings of self-worth. In other words, it comes from loving and appreciating yourself and from managing your own energetic vibrations. Knowing we are equal to all others allows for more open conversations. Just as we have begun to understand ourselves, we can now understand others.

People like to be understood and heard, so show a little non-judgmental curiosity. Also, a little empathy goes a long way in building bonds. Don't feel, like I did in the past, that asking questions is an infringement. Frankly, I am still not great at this. But I do have the skills and confidence to practice asking questions until it becomes more natural. Changing my infringement belief and coming from a place of self-worth were prerequisites for this growth potential.

You will undoubtedly have conversations that are more difficult than this example. Still, the process is basically the same: come from a place of self-worth, ask clarifying questions, and maintain awareness.

Maintaining alignment is key to avoid harmful reactions during difficult conversations. If another participant is aggressive, acknowledging their perspective may help. If you are the agitated one, know that strong emotions are part of the human experience. Perhaps it would be good to remove yourself from the situation with an acknowledgment that you are willing to come back to the conversation at a later time. It's okay to say, "I'm too angry to discuss this right now. Can we talk about it tomorrow night?" This allows you time to think about your reaction and align with how you truly feel, as well as, bring empathy and acknowledgment to how the other person feels.

Then, throughout the conversation, monitor your own energy level by scanning your physical body. A rising heart rate is an early sign of agitation that can lead to damaging reactions. Long, slow breaths will help maintain your awareness.

Now, observe the energy of the other participant(s). Pay more attention to their energy than their words. They may lash out with hurtful words. This is their ego looking for a reaction. In that moment, we don't know the life story behind their current perspective and what hurts may be causing their behavior. Try to step into their shoes and refrain from judging. It can never hurt to hold space, or be present in the moment for the person, without a personal agenda or attachment to the outcome.

As we become better at managing our vibrations and awareness, we can't help but become a positive influence on those around us. We will begin to attract people and situations that are more enjoyable.

Brian Seth Hurst uses a practical method for framing the direction of conversations. Early in the discussion, he suggests asking the other person, "What do you want from me in this conversation?" or "What would you like me to do with this information?" They may just want to be heard, or maybe they want your opinion or assistance in "fixing" something. If we try to fix something when they just want to feel understood, our response will not be received well.

After understanding their intent, we have a choice to participate or not. We do not have to engage in every conversation. For example, if your mom is complaining about her friend's bad manners for the fifteenth time, you can politely tell her that this is not a conversation you care to be a part of. Setting appropriate boundaries is a critical, yet often overlooked component to managing our own vibrations. This seems especially true for the "givers" of the world.

Also be clear about what you want out of conversations. Knowing what you want allows you to share that clarity with other participants. Do you want their assistance, opinion, or just to be heard?

Brian's final suggestion on this topic is to ask, "What am I learning from this?" This surrounds even unpleasant experiences with an awareness of the positives. Focusing on the positives is nothing more than a habit. Our habit can be to focus on the negatives and complain, or to focus on the positives. Our task is to habitually focus on the positive, and the Law of Attraction will dictate that more positive experiences come our way.

The combination of self-worth, monitoring energy levels, and practical conversation tools can dramatically change how you are perceived in the world, how effectively you communicate, and how much the world opens to you. Above all, when dealing with others, always offer love and compassion. The softness of love, much like that of water, can conquer all hard things.

In the following reading, Holly Burns helped a client with issues regarding conversations with others. *Permission has been granted to share all the readings included in this book and details have been changed to protect the participants' identities.*

Reading

Holly's client asked for a general reading. The message provided illustrates some of the concepts discussed in this chapter. Here is what Holly and the Elders had to say:

The first thing the Elders said was, "Every action relates to the reality you are creating around you." They were talking specifically about how you respond to other people. Someone around you is not behaving in a way that pleases you. You can respond to them by feeling upset and spending energy on how you wish they were behaving differently. Or you can stay up on a higher frequency of love for everything in the Universe, including them. Don't get pulled out of your high frequency by reacting to your surroundings.

Also, the fact that you got hurt by their words in the first place is an indication that you were not on your highest frequency at that moment. If you were, it would be impossible for you to feel that emotion. You would see things from an entirely different point of view. You would start to see that person's heartache piercing through their words and actions, which have nothing to do with you and everything to do with them and where they are now.

To solidify this frequency of consciousness, start shifting yourself up to the frequency of love and keeping your heart as open as possible. Choose responses to those around you that offer them love. Always offer love and appreciation for those around you, no matter what. That in turn will start shifting you over to a reality where you do like their behaviors, because, once again, you are the start of everything in your reality.

So just offer those around you unconditional love. You might not like their behavior, but you will stop taking it personally and can stay up on your higher frequency. Offer them mercy for the heartache and misalignment they are feeling in those moments. They, in turn, will allow more love into their Souls from the love you give them. They are only asking for love when they are behaving badly. They are feeling unloved from something going on in their lives and are acting out their own unhappiness.

CONTRAST

It takes darkness to be aware of the light.

~Treasure Tatum*

"Contrast" is something that conflicts with our desires. By this definition, contrast is an important element of creation on this planet. Imagine sitting up in heaven where everything is perfect. But what does perfect feel like if we have nothing to compare it to? Perfect becomes average or mundane. Average is fine, but it certainly does not inspire growth. We came to this planet to grow and expand, knowing that an environment full of contrast would stimulate that growth. From that higher perspective, contrast doesn't sound so bad. Down here on Earth, it means getting something we don't want. How fun is that? I believe God created us in a world of duality so we can discover who we really are, and through us, God can experience Himself/Herself.

What we do with contrast can be the difference between a miserable life and a happy life. We can choose to focus on the negative aspects of our life and attract more of the same. Or, we can use contrast to cause us to focus on what we would like better.

This pivoting action takes mental discipline and practice. It requires enough awareness to observe what we don't appreciate without reacting to it. Instead, we turn toward thoughts and feelings of what we do enjoy. Obstacles in the form of contrast are the self-correcting mechanism of the Universe. If we ignore the little signs, we risk veering too far off our path. A crisis may then be required to get our attention. Obstacles are not opposing us; on the contrary, they are redirecting us back to the flow.

Think of them as bumpers on a bowling alley. Even when one is in the flow, contrast is just a normal part of the process. It cannot be overstated how important it is to retrain our minds to react differently to contrast.

Here is a real-world example. Recently, I had taken a new job. After a month, the insanity at this new place was shocking. The environment could provide daily inspiration for the sitcom *The Office*, except this wasn't funny. Depression set in. The reason for my depression can be explained by my focus on the negatives. It doesn't matter if my negative thoughts were justified. We can choose to be right or to be happy. I allowed my negative thoughts to take me out of the flow. My emotions should have been my first clue about the direction of my focus.

Finally, I had enough. I consciously demanded to the Universe, "I am not going to let a job dictate my happiness ever again!" I had wasted too many years hating my jobs or my bosses. Enough was enough.

I consciously started focusing on the positives: my coworkers were great, people I loved lived nearby, my work schedule was flexible, there were no sales goals, I had time to devote to myself, the area was beautiful. A morning practice of listening to guided meditations and doing yoga contributed to my turnaround. Guided meditations can be a less-resistant way out of dark places compared to self-directed meditation. One just sits back and enjoys the ride, rather than pulling ourselves out of a hole.

My statement to the Universe was heard loud and clear. By pivoting my focus, I began what proved to be the most productive period of my life. I became self-empowered and happy. I learned to manifest abundance, communicate with the Universe, and listen to my higher self. I finally learned how to navigate life. And I wrote this book!

There is so much to take away from this story. First, I kept attracting bad jobs because every time I left a job, I still hated it. This is an example of "wherever you go, there you are." We must get happy with where we are now before anything will change. Second, great desire has immense energy behind it. I was not casually thinking about how my life could be better. I demanded that it become better. Use the power of desire wisely and with positive intent. Third, every conversation in our head is a conversation with the Universe. Negative or positive, it is sending a vibrational request that is sure to be answered. Fourth, we are empowered to change our lives by being aware of our thoughts, feelings, and vibrations, and then consciously redirecting or focusing them.

Interestingly, our higher selves will sometimes direct us toward challenges knowing that they will provide the stimulation to drive us toward our desires. Focusing on the positives will leverage the situation for our own good. We know we are going to have contrast in this life, so we might as well become masters at working with it. When life throws a fastball at you, use that force to knock it out of the park!

Next is a reading from Holly expanding on the topic of contrast.

Reading

Holly's client asked about the difficulties in his current job search. This is what followed:

The Elders are saying you need to shift your reactions. They said you are currently viewing your "failed" job applications from the perspective of "okay, you're not hiring me, and you don't want me."

Instead, they want you to see everything from this perspective: My flow knows precisely where I am supposed to go next and will lead me right to it. If a job is my job, then I'll be hired. If it isn't, then I know I had that experience for some reason that will help me get the job that is mine.

When you shift over to trusting the Universal flow, suddenly you let in a flood of excitement for what is coming to you. You feel the calling to expand yourself and look for better opportunities, and you know it's there, just around the bend. You are enjoying the experience of finding your way to something better. You are so pumped that you will soon have a better experience with better pay, and you are so excited to live that reality. You just can't wait for it to get here!

Feel the difference? The latter perspective has a lot more forward momentum and will get you to the results you want about three times as fast!

It's all about your reactions to what others are doing. Don't jump out of a high vibration and get upset looking at a situation that didn't go the way you thought it should go. Remain on the high frequency of the new job. Find the feeling of it and relish in that success. By doing that, you are creating that. Alternatively, by getting frustrated about what's not happening (that is how you are currently choosing to react to it), you are creating more of that. That slows down your progress.

They say to ask your inner heart, "Am I never going to get another job; am I going to have to stay where I am forever?" No, you know that is not true. Your inner self is telling you that there is something better out there. So just trust a little longer and understand what you don't get is sometimes leading you right to something way better instead!

While I was still figuring out the rules on this planet, Holly did a similar reading for me. Work was frustrating, my relationship was struggling, and money was a frequent worry.

Highlighting the art of pivoting, she said, "You are focusing on the three cups turned over, or spilled, in front of you, and you are completely missing the cups filled up right behind you. Two of these cups represent windfalls of abundance. Turn toward those cups!"

When something is not working, it tends to get our full attention. Back off your attention from those areas and concentrate more intently on the things that you are grateful for, including those things that haven't even manifested yet. Focusing on "the cups behind me" has proven to be one of the most successful techniques in my toolbox.

Finally, if a problem seems too big, give it to your team of Spirit Guides and/or God. They will gladly take them. Use them as your team of assistants to delegate tasks at any time.

Affirmations

Contrast pushes me to new heights.

Going within, I find the answers to all my obstacles.

I don't take thoughts too seriously—mine or other people's.

I always offer love and appreciation.

I love being surrounded by spiritually awakened people.

I am the start of everything in my reality.

With ease, I allow my path to rise up before me.

My flow takes me exactly where I'm supposed to go.

Where my focus goes, my fortune flows.

Success is seeking me out.

Everything is going to be better than I thought.

The Universe is knocking itself out to help me.

My vibration is making bigger leaps each and every day.

My vibration never falls back down; it just goes higher and higher.

I am doing extremely well.

NATURE

Nature's peace will flow into you as sunshine flows into trees.

~John Muir

Nature has always been a part of my life. Growing up in sparsely populated South Dakota near the confluence of the small, muddy Bad River, and the more massive Missouri River, there were endless opportunities to escape.

Sometimes we neighborhood kids would pack our backpacks with saltine crackers and a bottle of water and go on day-long hikes through the hills that overlooked the Missouri. More frequently, I spent solitary hours on the banks of the Bad River hoping something would bite my hook, a rare occurrence.

One time, at about four years of age, my boredom must have gotten the best of me as I pestered my mom to a rarely seen level of frustration. As she chased me for a presumed punishment, I darted out the front door and into the woods along the river across the street. I spent most of the day there. Mom was in a much better mood when I got home, and so was I. Not a word of our prior encounter was mentioned. I always appreciated that nature would take care of me when called upon.

I had never really acknowledged my relationship with nature, however, until I was in my teens. My oldest brother took me deer hunting along beautiful Lake Oahe (pronounced O-ah-HE). As I took off stomping into the hills, he advised, "Nature moves at a slower pace. Slow your breathing and your pace." Following his suggestion, I began to sense a calmness all around. I had never stopped to think that nature had a pace. Doesn't that almost imply a consciousness? It sure seemed so on that day, as I was now surrounded by an awareness or presence.

Adopt the pace of nature; her secret is patience.

~Ralph Waldo Emerson*

The lesson carried into my future fishing trips, which took on new meaning as I observed the river. It really had been a companion of mine for many years, despite my ignorance. Fishing seemed like merely an excuse to spend hours sitting by the river.

When I met my significant other, I was glad to hear that she also considered herself to be a "river rat," as she grew up on the Wisconsin River. Some may use the term as a slight, but we shared the connotation that it represents the vitality and experiences that one gains from growing up near the river.

In this chapter, I want to briefly discuss two specific aspects of nature: trees and water. Trees teach us to be still, observe, and just *be*. Trees aren't trying to be anything other than what they are. They start out as seeds and become the beautiful statues that they are, not by trying to be something, but just by being who they are. They *are* beautiful. They don't have to try to be beautiful. The same can be said of us.

Trees also teach us about navigating adversity. When the winds blow, they are resilient yet flexible. In fact, the winds help to strengthen the tree, just as our obstacles can be viewed as stepping-stones to a better us. Too much rigidity and we break.

Then, there is seasonality. During the summer, trees provide shade. Come autumn, they naturally release their leaves. They understand that the fallen leaves will enrich the soil for future generations. Just as they received nutrients from the fertile soil as seedlings, they now give back. This is the flow of life. We will have seasons, and eventually, these bodies we reside in will die.

Praise and blame, gain and loss, pleasure and sorrow come and go like the wind. To be happy, rest like a giant tree in the midst of them all.

~Buddha*

Here's a little exercise to test and increase your awareness. Think of a place you frequently walk outside. Maybe it's in a park, or perhaps around your house. Can you recall how many trees or bushes there are in that area? Some may have a hard time knowing how many trees are along the street on the block in front of their house. Yet you have driven or walked by there hundreds of times.

Next time you go outside, notice the number and placement of the trees. See how the branches of separate trees intertwine in harmony as they seek the sun's light. Notice how the bushes are placed relative to the trees. Observe how the grass spreads to fill in the gaps. Nature has a way of perfectly orchestrating the layout of its species. Even in a tangled forest, the mess has a sense of beauty to it. Again, the same can be said of us.

Now, let's get even more intimate. Pick a tree you see frequently. Sit and spend ten minutes observing the tree and being with the tree. Maybe it is the one right off your front steps. Have you ever become fully aware of it? How do its branches spread out? What do the leaves or buds look like at this time of year? Does the trunk twist, or does the bark have any unique characteristics? Have you noticed this before, or have you always walked by the tree without paying much attention? Can you feel any energy radiating from the tree? There is so much detail to observe. As you repeat this visit, more will come to you. Next time you walk by, do you think your awareness of the tree will have changed, or will you blindly pass by it again?

Be still and the Earth will speak to you.
~Navajo Proverb

We do the same thing with people we pass every day. We go by each other without even giving an opening. Try giving friendly smiles to strangers as you are walking. How many people will not even acknowledge or see you? Once you connect with someone, whether it is through a smile or a "Hello," you tend to acknowledge them more at future encounters. This can be the opening for a friendship.

In my early 40s, I took an earth medicine class to heighten my understanding of nature. The biggest takeaway from these lessons was that "if you honor nature, nature will honor you." Isn't this true for all relationships? Building relationships, with nature or people, requires patience, attention, and kindness.

Those who honor me, I will honor.
~1 Samuel 2:30

Even small amounts of time in nature can positively impact our mental and physical health. Connecting with the Earth can literally ground us. We are energetic beings. If you ever have the urge to go outside, follow that intuition. Your body is telling you that it could use some grounding.

As you sit or stand in nature, picture the Earth's energy flowing from your feet, up your legs, through your trunk, and eventually into your head. The energy knows exactly where to go and how to heal. It will bring you back to a stillness, the stillness that is really you. Thank Gaia for the healing. She is always there for you. As a variation of this experience, you may want to try lying on the ground for a more bath-like experience. As you do this, notice how supported you are in every way.

Water is another symbolic aspect of nature. For comments on that, I can do no better than Lao Tzu, a sixth-century B.C.E. Chinese philosopher and author of the *Tao Te Ching*.

Nothing in the world is softer and weaker than water. But for attacking the hard, the unyielding, nothing can surpass it. There is nothing like it.

~Lao Tzu

Of course, Lao Tzu is not merely referring to the physical characteristics of water. He is speaking metaphorically about the mental aspects of non-resistance. When I read the quote, I can't help but think of Martin Luther King, Jr. His use of love to overcome hatred is a perfect example of Lao Tzu's philosophy.

We humans are not only connected to one another, but we are also connected with the Earth and all of its inhabitants. Honor these relationships and allow nature's energy to heal us and teach us. This is why I refer to nature as my church.

Meditation

Below is a short meditation that Staci Wells taught me. This meditation shows that even picturing nature can have positive effects. Say it multiple times throughout your day to quiet your mind.

Touch the index finger and thumb together on each of your hands.

Close your eyes.

Picture a very serene, deep, glass-like mountain lake.

Repeat the saying "mind like calm water" three times.

Let the image bring stillness to your mind and heart.

Allow your body to relax and feel the noise of your day subside.

TWO MOST POWERFUL PHRASES

*By your words you will be acquitted, and by your words
you will be condemned.*

~Matthew 12:37

We have discussed a lot about how thoughts and feelings possess creation energy. And if that is true, it only makes sense that spoken words are especially creative.

In general, conversations deserve proper care and mindfulness. When you catch yourself saying negative things, correct them with positive declarations. For example, saying something as simple as "traffic will probably be bad again" should be corrected unless you want to encounter delays. Changing the statement to "I expect smooth and easy travels," and more importantly, believing it, sends a much different energy to the Universe. On most lengthy motorcycle or car trips, I go a step further and picture myself comfortably at my destination.

More specifically, there are two creative phrases that deserve a more detailed explanation. These phrases are:

Thank You

and

I Am

Neither of these phrases should surprise you, as they have been repeated by inspirational leaders throughout time. These phrases need to be in our "feel-good" toolbox and part of our daily practice. Let's briefly address each one separately.

Thank You

"Thank you" is one of the greatest prayers. It is a statement of appreciation. When we are in appreciation, we cannot simultaneously be focused on negative thoughts. These words are the flowers that crowd out the weeds in the garden of your Soul.

Focusing on things you appreciate creates a single-eyed view. Let "thank you" be your first and last prayer of every day, but don't stop there. Make it an exercise as you go through your day to find things you appreciate.

When it comes to these tools, I'm not even close to perfect, but I try to keep them in my back pocket and work with them as often as possible. For example, walking into work is a great time to notice all the beautiful trees, flowers, and landscaping. Notice any wildlife. Appreciate the architecture, the weather, and whatever else you can find. Use this short stroll as an opportunity to seek out beauty and say "thank you." Waiting in line at the grocery store provides another perfect opportunity. Be thankful for the patient cashiers, notice the people who are smiling, appreciate the fact that you can simply go to a store and load up on food. Send up a quick prayer by saying "thank you." These are not just nice words you are reading; these are simple action items. Practice and notice what happens. Perhaps instead of leaving the grocery store stressed, you might leave with a sense of peace.

Right now, think of something you truly appreciate. Hold it in your mind's eye for a moment, and say "thank you." Notice the energy in your body after you say the words. Can you feel the vibrational shift? Two simple words, yet they are moving the energy throughout your body. Congratulations on being aware of your energy and your ability to control your vibrations. See how powerful you are? You are becoming an intentional creator!

"Thank you" also sends energy into the Universe. All energy you send out comes back. Look for opportunities to say "thank you" and to send love.

Make this a regular habit. It is solely up to you to change your habits. Be thankful that you are aware. Be thankful that you have the power to change your life. Be thankful for the abundance that is coming your way, seen and unseen, as a result of your efforts. Be thankful you live in such an exciting Universe where all of this is possible. Who knew it was so magical? This is the way it works. Thank you.

You can also be thankful for you. Rap musician, Snoop Dogg had this to say when his star was added to the Hollywood Walk of Fame:

> *"Last but not least, I want to thank me... I want to thank me for believing in me. ... I want to thank me for never quitting. I want to thank me for always being a giver and trying to give more than I receive.*
> *I want to thank me for trying to do more right than wrong;*
> *I want to thank me for just being me at all times."*

Finally, say thank you for things that don't appear to be working in your favor. The Universe works in mysterious and indirect ways, but it is always working in your favor. It is much wiser than any of us. Is there a tough situation or circumstance you want to dissolve? What can you take from that situation? Say "thank you," and mean it.

> *The quickest path from need to abundance is gratitude.*
> ~Unknown

Finally, a great healing practice is to send love and gratitude to the people who represent your biggest challenges. Love dissolves all. While this may have positive benefits for our "enemies," the biggest impact will be on our own vibration. Once again, you can't be hating while you are loving. Our greatest challengers bring us our greatest rewards.

I Am

While "thank you" may be one of the most powerful prayers, "I am" might carry the most creation power. There are no more important words than the words you speak to and for yourself. The fact that you speak more to yourself than anyone else only adds to the significance of these conversations. As you will discover in later chapters, the Universe hears all things we tell ourselves, so choose your comments wisely!

Personally, I like to use this creative force by writing a string of "I am" phrases in a journal or notebook to spiral myself into a better feeling state. Later, you can either write new ones or read past entries, depending on your mood. Tailor these to your current needs, whether they are financial, romantic, or just general concerns that you may be having. Let me provide a couple examples of these rants. This first one I created for professional/abundance purposes:

I Am Valuable

I am extremely valuable, and the Universe recognizes that value.

I am compensated for the extreme value I bring to the Universe.

I am fully supported in every facet of my life.

I am bringing the greatest value by being myself.

I am creating a life in which my ideas are valued and respected.

I am valued and respected for my forward thinking, pioneering, and desire to contribute.

I am compensated for just being me.

I am allowing all the income I need to come my way.

I am appreciated, loved, and valued for who I am.

I am creating, manifesting, and sharing effortlessly.

I am allowing abundance to come in ways seen and unseen.

I am a best-selling author.

I am releasing all fears, as I move forward with certainty.

I am destined to make all my dreams come true.

I am living a fun, easy, joyful life.

I am free to follow my joy wherever it may lead me.

I am surrounded by beautiful, intelligent, happy, like-minded people.

I am expecting to see beautiful people, places, and things.

I am a seer of beauty.

I am abundant. I am loved. I have purpose. I am guided.

I am thinking bigger, better, more clearly, and more often.

I am a master allower and a master creator.

I am a magician, and nothing can stop my magical ass!

I am rockin' this entire life.

I am knocking it out of the park.

I am complete and confident in every aspect of my life.

We can also work with "I am" in a simple format with great power. As you go through all the things you are, begin to realize that "I am" is all-encompassing. I end the list simply with "I am," knowing those two words encapsulate all the prior statements. It represents total being and consciousness and provides a glimpse into "all that is" and all that I am—the oneness of the Universe. See if you can tap into this feeling, too. Practice this simple exercise as often as possible. Eventually, you may be able to state the words "I am," and that will be all you need.

I am

I am safe.

I am secure.

I am abundant.

I am healthy.

I am wealthy.

I am happy.

I am loving.

I am kind.

I am compassionate.

I am supported.

I am guided.

I am resilient.

I am smart.

I am friendly.

I am generous.

I am gregarious.

I am sensitive.

I am funny.

I am sexy.

I am a teacher.

I am rich.

I am a creator.

I am adventurous.

I am disciplined.

I am resourceful.

I am successful.

I am beautiful.

I am passionate.

I am communicative.

I am understanding.

I am strong.

I am powerful.

I am unlimited.

I am trusting.

I am allowing.

I am appreciative.

I am relaxed.

I am caring.

I am valued.

I am cherished.

I am free.

I am calm.

I am peaceful.

I am aware.

I am the light.

I am loved.

I am love.

I am.

SECTION TWO
Creating

In Section One, we removed beliefs, thoughts, and habits that hinder the creation process. In other words, we cleared the ground for our garden. In this section, we'll fine-tune working with the more subtle and positive vibrations. Staying in the flow at higher levels of vibration can require different tools than those used in the clearing phase. This is where we plant the seeds, provide fertilizer, and most importantly, allow our garden to spring to life. While we may have some general ideas about how our garden will look in the end, the truly magical part is that the beauty will be somewhat of a surprise. It will likely be far greater and come in different forms than we imagined. Holly and the Elders will play a much bigger role in this section.

HUNCHING

Have a mind that is open to everything and attached to nothing.

~Tilopa*

Hunching is a way of sniffing around for the path of least resistance. The Universe doesn't give you something on a silver platter. Sometimes you have to feel your way. Let's use some stories to get the point across.

As I was writing this book, my significant other and I were planning a Caribbean vacation for us and our five boys for spring break. Yes, you read that right, five boys. It had been a long time since we had done anything nice together, and they were getting older—their ages ranged from 15 to 22 at the time. We knew that a few of them would be out on their own soon, and the opportunities to do something together would only get more complicated.

We tried to arrange a trip to Punta Cana utilizing some benefits from a vacation package we purchased a year earlier. As one typically discovers with vacation "deals," the restrictions on the package made it next to impossible to use. We checked several options in various locations, but eventually gave up. My significant other and her boys found a trip to Florida, and my oldest boy planned a car trip across the country with his college friends.

That left my younger son and me to come up with something. In discussing details, it became apparent that his spring break was actually a week after everyone else's. His college's website had not been updated after a scheduling change, so we didn't know that when we started making plans. Good thing we couldn't purchase the Punta Cana trip, or we would have lost his plane fare!

The first lesson here is that even when it appears things aren't working out, know that they are always working out for you. Second, don't force things. If they don't fall into place easily, they probably aren't meant to be.

Unfortunately, I was unable to change my vacation dates to match his spring break due to my work schedule. Now, he was going to seek out other options. I said "unfortunately" to start this paragraph, but in truth I could sense that I was supposed to go on this trip alone. Try not to judge circumstances. From our limited perspective, we never really know whether something is good or bad.

This left me with several options, and I tried to open up to all the possibilities. First, I could cancel my vacation time and save it for later. I could also rent a cheap condo in northern Wisconsin at a small ski resort. The quiet time would be good for my book-writing efforts. I could also stay home and use my vacation time to write, but I'm not a big believer in using vacation time in the winter to stick around the house.

Another option would be to attend the college wrestling championships in Pittsburgh. My significant other's sister lives there, so lodging would be free. Attending the wrestling championships was a bucket list item I crossed off my list a couple of years ago. I would love to go again, but I had tentatively planned to go next year when they would be in nearby Minneapolis.

Finally, I have always wanted to go to Park City, Utah, to enjoy the world-class skiing. I have frequently shopped for dream houses there on the Internet and loved the thought of living in that natural playground. This would be a much more expensive trip, and thus, less practical. Also, I had never taken a big trip like that by myself, so the thought seemed somewhat odd. However, I have learned that if you dream of a particular place, you need to go see it and feel it.

I meditated for a solution for a couple days and was starting to stress about it. Time was running short. None of the options jumped out at me. That's when I realized that I needed to give it space. Solutions always come. They ALWAYS come. Just give the problem up; give it to God or the Universe.

> *Face a situation fearlessly, and there is no situation to face;*
> *it falls by its own weight.*
>
> ~Florence Scovel Shinn

The next night, I woke up around 2 AM, grabbed my cell phone and did a quick Internet search for rent-by-owner units in Utah. I'm not sure what prompted me to do this. Anyway, I found a place that seemed to have the right vibes for my getaway and my writing. It was at the opening of the canyon that was home to some ski resorts and backed up to a beautiful mountain creek. The owner was an interior designer and master gardener, so the place was stunning inside and out. I could feel myself getting excited—and to my credit, I noticed that. I did some trip planning the next day and found some deals on ski passes, rental vehicles, and airfare. Everything fell together easily. Now, I was really excited. This would be just what I needed! It is amazing how solutions come when you take the pressure off.

Did you notice the difference between planning the Utah trip versus the Punta Cana trip? When things are clicking and feel right, go with the flow. When every step seems to be a struggle, back off.

Before we move on with this story, it is important to discuss the topic of numbers briefly. The Universe often speaks through numbers, if you pay attention. Often, specific numbers will appear as commentary on the thoughts currently running through my head. Usually, I want to see a number three times before I assign any significance to it. I do make exceptions, though. For example, a couple of weeks before planning my trip, I saw two cars in front of me at a stop light that both had 648 on their license plates. While highly improbable, it still did not meet my requirement of three sightings. As I glanced up ahead to the next row of cars, I was given confirmation that I needed to pay attention to the number.

This confirmation came on a third license plate in the form of my own personal number that the Universe often uses to wink at me. My number is 56 (or sometimes 156). It was my old high school football number and has been very prevalent in my life the past few years.

Joanne Walmsley has a website called Sacred Scribes (sacredscribes.blogspot.com) that interprets angel numbers into the thousands. With the two cars in front of me in mind, I went to her site to look up the meaning of 648. The interpretation I found gave me the nudge to start writing this book. As you start practicing with this form of communication, you will be amazed at how personal and timely the messages can be.

In case you are curious, the meaning of 648 included this sentence: "If you are feeling inclined to begin, pursue or expand a spiritually-based practice, profession or career, or any business or money-making venture that involves helping and serving others, Angel Number 648 can suggest that it is an auspicious time to begin as you will find long-term success and personal fulfillment helping others and serving your Soul's mission."

Let's get back to my vacation. After making all the arrangements that day, the Universe began to immediately applaud my efforts through numerical signs. Leaving the parking lot at work to head home, the opposing car across the street had 56 on the license place, as did two more within the next block.

Now, the odds of seeing a 56 on a license plate with three numbers (the other three characters are typically letters in Wisconsin) are two in 999. It could be x56 or 56x, with x being any other number. So, the odds that I saw three of them in row would be (2/999) * (2/999) * (2/999), or approximately 0.0000008% for you math majors. Later that night, as I drove my son on an errand, I saw no fewer than ten 56s on license plates. The Universe was pleased with my decision to go to Utah.

It gets better. The night before at 2 AM, I asked the Universe to show "313" in the morning if this trip was meant to be. This was a purely random number that popped into my head. I knew seeing that specific number would be a clear sign. The number did not appear on the way to work, but as I was running errands that evening, I saw it! Across the intersection at a red light, a license plate with 313 stared back at me! I had forgotten that I had even asked for the sign. Now, a skeptic could easily say that it was a coincidence. But guess what I found on the license plate on the car immediately after the 313 car, 56!

The point of my story is not necessarily about numbers; it is about making decisions and following our feelings. I believe that the Universe could have provided the 313 first thing the next morning as requested, but instead I was given an invaluable lesson to give space for solutions, emotionally weigh the options, and follow my feelings. When the Universe gave the confirmation with the 313 and 56 late in the day, it was a way of saying, "Well done. You are on the right path and are learning how to make decisions." Learning to live in this manner will change your life.

I thought the story of my Utah trip would end there, but it was just beginning.

Waiting at the airport, I began reviewing my trip information. My flight number was 1562. And the house number where I would stay was 3656. Two more 56s to confirm that I was precisely on the right path.

The second day in Utah, I skied at Solitude Mountain Resort. It was a beautiful sunny day with no lines at the chairlifts, despite it being a Sunday during spring break. I was able to soak in nature's beauty, especially while riding the chairlifts to the top of the mountain. You can meet many friendly people on the chairlifts willing to share stories and tips for enjoying the local community. I had some of those encounters, but I also was able to have many solo trips that allowed for perfect segments of meditation. Many ideas for this book came during these trips to the top. I could feel myself downloading information. This book was not so much being written by me, but through me. By the end of the day, I was feeling very grateful for the experience, knowing full well that this was where I was supposed to be.

Exiting the parking lot to head home, I asked the Universe/ Spirit Guides if they had a good time. The Universe loves communication and enjoys sharing our adventures. We are never truly alone. After posing this question, I noticed a license plate on a parked car about three spots up on my right. The license plate had the number 1056 on it. The steady communication with the Universe was beginning to floor me. I will not bore you with all the numerical occurrences those few days, but it was apparent that I had company that entire trip. I felt so blessed for the guidance, attention, and winks.

Neal Zealand Story

One final lesson and blessing came to me on my last day of skiing. As I waited in line for the gondola to make its first trip to the summit, an older man invited me to ski with him.

Neal from New Zealand, or Neal Zealand as his friends called him, was a fascinating man who had lived about 150 years' worth of experiences during his 75 years on this planet. While his 5'5", 140-pound frame was not intimidating, his presence was something to behold. Neal had been a professional musician, an artist with published books, a restorer of commercial real estate, and an electrician, among other things. It was apparent that Neal was an expert "huncher." He followed his joy and instincts without paying heed to fear or doubt.

Neal had been coming to Snowbird for 40 years, and relayed much of the history of the place. I tend to avoid overly talkative people, but there was something different about Neal.

During the first two runs, Neal began giving many uninvited skiing pointers to me. At first, I was wondering how many runs I should do before I ditch this guy, but his suggestions were resulting in quick improvements in my ability. Also, it was hard not to warm up to his charismatic personality. I had been skiing for close to 40 years, but never had any lessons. Apparently, it showed.

Now, Neal was not your average 75-year-old skier. I would struggle to keep up with him down the runs and never once beat him to the bottom. As it turns out, Neal has skied with the best extreme skiers in the world and been on helicopter trips to help film the action shots.

One particular time, the helicopter was carrying too much weight and was above its rated altitude. After making a stop on a peak, the pilot attempted to lift off. Not getting anywhere, he told the crew to hang on as he tilted the propeller to push them forward…headfirst off a cliff. The helicopter nose-dived to gain airspeed, but eventually leveled off. The star skier, squeezed in the back with no seat belt, was thrown forward through the cabin during the maneuver. Fortunately, the others were able to impede his flight before he could crash into the helicopter's control panel.

Before his wild ski adventure stories, Neal told me about his ski lessons a couple of years ago at the age of 73. Ski lessons at age 73, for an expert skier? Personally, I thought I was too old for my first lesson at age 50.

Neal was a living example of staying humble enough to keep learning throughout life. Relinquishing what you think you know creates an opening and allows new perspectives to filter in. In every aspect of our lives, seek to eliminate the restrictions imposed by beliefs, fears, ego, and ignorance.

"Humility engenders learning because it beats back the arrogance that puts blinders on. It leaves you open for truths to reveal themselves. You don't stand in your own way."
~Wynton Marsalis

I am glad I did not turn down the opportunity to learn from Neal, despite my early egotistical thought of "who is this guy?" This entire encounter, in fact my entire trip to Utah, was the result of "hunching" and following my intuition. Intuition is a spiritual faculty that becomes stronger the more you use it. To use it, still your reasoning mind and trust that the Universe knows exactly where you want to go.

Neal and I packed more ski runs into three hours than I ever had before. But skiing had very little to do with our encounter. The bonus was that I now had another chapter for my book!

Affirmations

I give space for perfect solutions to come.

My spaciousness is the birthplace of perfect solutions.

I follow my leads with great excitement.

It is fun to follow the leads of the Universe.

I never miss a lead.

The Universe gives me very clear leads that I cannot miss.

I am an allower of perfect solutions.

I allow great solutions, and great solutions are seeking me.

I expect great things to come to me.

Perfect things come to me in perfect ways.

Miracles happen all the time, even now.

I allow miracles quickly and effortlessly.

It has to come easy, because it can't come hard.

I ease my way into perfect solutions.

There are many possible solutions, and the best ones find their way to me.

My path will find me; I do not need to find it.

I allow solutions that are better than I ever could have imagined.

CONNECTING THE DOTS

I have been a seeker and still am, but I stopped asking books and the stars. I started listening to the teaching of my Soul.

~Rumi*

In June 2005, Steve Jobs, the co-founder of Apple Inc., gave a famous speech to the graduating class of Stanford University. Jobs had been diagnosed with terminal cancer a year earlier. The 15-minute speech was impactful, and it touched on a few key points of this book.

The first point is that the "dots" in life will connect. In his speech, Jobs stated, "You can't connect the dots looking forward; you can only connect them looking backward. Trust that the dots will somehow connect in your future. You have to trust in something—your gut, destiny, life, karma, whatever. This approach has never let me down, and it has made all the difference in my life."

As you get older, you will notice that, from our human perspective, things *usually* work out. From a Soul perspective, they *always* work out. When encountering significant crossroads in life, it is easy to become stressed worrying about outcomes. Everything seems to hinge on the next result.

I believe we have a divine path. While we have many choices on this path, there are certain anchoring points to guide us along the way. When Jobs stated that we cannot connect the dots going forward, I believe he meant that we cannot *see* how they connect looking forward, but he did know how to ensure that they connect. "Trust in something," and as you'll soon see, follow your bliss.

At the age of 30, Jobs was fired from Apple—the company he started. He described his feelings at the time: "I was a very public failure, and I even thought about running away from the valley. But something slowly began to dawn on me—I still loved what I did. The turn of events at Apple had not changed that one bit. I had been rejected, but I was still in love. And so I decided to start over. I didn't see it then, but it turned out that getting fired from Apple was the best thing that could have ever happened to me. The heaviness of being successful was replaced by the lightness of being a beginner again, less sure about everything. It freed me to enter one of the most creative periods of my life...."

This is my secret: I don't mind what happens.
~Jiddu Krishnamurti

In his book, *A Weekend with 'a' Drunken Leprechaun*, Klaus Joehle captures a similar feeling:

*"Well I want something to do, to create, to achieve, to whatever...Something I can't get enough of. You know something that I can't wait to get up in the morning to do, something I can't get enough of, something that brings me joy and makes my heart sing. It could be anything, could be more than one thing but something that grabs me. Even a job, if it grabs me so that I could hardly wait to get there. Something that makes me feel good, allows me to be me, gives me freedom to grow and expand, something that grasps my heart, my joy, my excitement and leads me down the path to more joyful things, exciting challenges and challenging things. Barely stopping to take a breath I continued. I need a new journey a new destination, I want to grow to be or become, tread a new path, see what I haven't seen be what I haven't been ask what I haven't asked dare to what I haven't dared to...I don't even think it is so much a physical thing or mental it's just sort of unlearning some of what I learned. It's being happy, while I am happy but I want something to do that creates even more. ... **Doing it for the joy of doing it, not for any other reason.**"*

Both men were describing the process of following their joy. Following his joy allowed Jobs to connect the next dots after being fired. He had a couple of successful ventures after being fired, one of which was later bought by Apple. Jobs returned to Apple during that acquisition and is widely credited with saving the company. His other venture was the animated film company Pixar.

When Jobs was fired, he did not know what the next dot was, but he knew to follow his passion. Not knowing the next dot makes life exciting. If we simply follow the path that brings us joy, the dots will connect in the most joyous way possible. Joy begets more joy.

If you want to take an alternative route, go ahead and worry about something. Worrying pinches the flow of life and takes you on unwanted detours (as we learned earlier, these obstacles contain a self-correcting mechanism in the form of contrast). However, you are destined to eventually succeed, whether in this life or a later one. You cannot get it wrong. Knowing you can't get it wrong, why not sit back and enjoy the journey? It really can be as simple as following your bliss.

"You just come to the point where you know you're getting it and are content with allowing it to be a surprise as to how and when. In many ways that's part of the fun."
~Klaus Joehle

Often, what we immediately judge as an adverse event turns into a blessing. Steve Jobs was initially devastated by losing his job, but eventually saw the gift that the situation presented. Jobs added, "I'm convinced that the only thing that kept me going was that I loved what I did. You've got to find what you love." In my life, divorce was the event that turned into my greatest blessing. It caused me to rethink everything, to humbly turn toward God, and open up to a new and exciting way of living. Don't second-guess God's plans!

Here's another quick personal story about not judging a situation by outward appearances: it was my last day of work before a vacation that would involve driving over two thousand miles to western Wyoming and back. On my way to work that morning, my pickup stalled going down the highway, and I coasted to the shoulder. I was able to restart the vehicle and limp to work and back home with a few more stalls and restarts. My first thought was that this was perfectly bad timing with my vacation looming.

After several calls, I found a dealership in a nearby town that could get my truck in the next day. Fortunately, they were able to have a part delivered that day and, after eight hours at the shop, I was on my way. The $700 repair was covered by warranty. If this had happened about 500 miles and one day later, the warranty would have expired due to mileage, and I would have been stranded in the middle of nowhere.

What I could have easily labeled as an unfortunate event turned out to be a big blessing. Make every attempt to never judge a situation. Remain calm and remain open to solutions. Things are always working out. There is a bigger plan at work. Remaining in the flow despite outward appearances allows for the plan to come to fruition in the most natural manner possible. In the words of Jobs, "Sometimes life hits you in the head with a brick. Don't lose faith."

The final point of Jobs' speech was to "Stay Hungry, Stay Foolish." Don't let fear keep you from following your passions.

The next chapter will expand on connecting the dots. We don't have to connect the dots in a forward-moving fashion, but can connect them by looking backward from a future perspective in what I call "feeling from the end."

FEELING FROM THE END

There is no stopping the man who can think from the end.
Nothing can stop him.

~Neville Goddard

Our current thoughts and feelings are always attracting our future external circumstances. Reacting to the current reality will only perpetuate more of the same. To get ahead of the curve, we must redirect our focus from the current situation and toward the desired condition. The key to this vision is that you can't just picture it, you must *feel* it. Feeling from the end will change our future realities, and it has the power to dramatically improve our lives.

Having wrestled hundreds of matches as a young athlete, I understood the strong correlation between my thoughts leading up to the competition and the results. Additionally, history books are filled with stories of incredibly successful athletes who have implemented the power of visualization. Whenever highly successful athletes are interviewed, pay attention. They speak differently and act differently. They carry themselves with confidence, like they know they have already won.

If we practice a feeling, the Universe will fill in the details in ways that are much better than we could have ever dreamed up. Don't get too specific about a vision. Practice desired feelings, with out focusing on envisioning specific outcomes. The element of feeling takes the top off the visualization process and makes life miraculous, as you will soon see.

This visualization process came to me shortly after I declared to the Universe that a job would no longer dictate my happiness.

If you recall, I started a process of meditation, yoga, and other "feel-good" practices to get out of my rut. This routine built a lot of positive momentum in my life within just two to three months. Good thoughts attracted more good thoughts, and soon I had strong momentum going.

My daily practice would get me into such a good feeling zone that I would just sit back and bask in the feeling for as long as it felt good. You will know when you get in that state. It's hard to describe, but it's a feeling that all is right and comfortable—so comfortable that you realize this feeling is all you really need. It is joy and a very powerful and creative state of mind. Spending 15 minutes each day in this state will change your life. Creating by this means is almost like becoming rich by getting a massage. If you make these processes part of your regular practice, you may not have to actually "work" another day in your life. The goal—to navigate life in the most joyous way possible.

Next is the visualization that I practice periodically.

Visualization

I am a major league baseball player, and I am up to bat. I see the pitcher throwing a fastball right down the middle of the plate. I take a swing with that perfect form where your hips come around first and your arms follow through, much like an easy golf stroke. My upward swing of the bat connects perfectly with the ball. I can feel that I hit it just right. You know that feeling, right? Sometimes I would repeat the swing in my head until the contact with the ball felt perfect. The strong pitch and my perfect swing do all the work. The ball explodes off the bat. Most home runs go just over the fence, or at most 50 rows into the seats. This ball is going up and over the upper deck, heading way outside the stadium. I TOTALLY KILLED IT!

The audience enters a stunned silence. No one has ever hit a ball anywhere close to that far. My teammates gather outside the dugout, looking on in silent disbelief. One commentator says, "I didn't see where the ball landed." His partner quietly replies, "It hasn't," as if he doesn't believe what he is saying. I toss my bat to the side and start jogging around the bases. I smilingly look to my teammates and shrug my shoulders as if to say, "How did that happen?" By the time I make it to third base, the silence of the stadium has broken into a loud roar. My teammates greet me as I approach home plate with hugs and high fives.

My next at-bat, I switch to batting left-handed. Yes, I'm that talented. The same thing happens. The perfect connection sends the ball out of the park, this time over right field. The crowd soon enters that same loud roar. There is less disbelief this time as my teammates immediately begin jumping around in excitement. "This is crazy!" they seem to be thinking. They put me on their shoulders and carry me around for a while. After I enter the dugout, the crowd demands that I come out for an encore celebration. I go out and give a wave to the highly energized fan base, indulging in their electric energy.

Now I am at the plate for my third and final at-bat. I switch back to batting right-handed this time. The umpire is starting to get suspicious that something fishy is going on. He takes a fresh ball out of his pocket and marks it with a red "X" to make sure I have not tampered with the ball. By this time, news has spread around the country and every televised game tunes in to watch me. I am playing in New York. Meanwhile, the grounds crew in Los Angeles watches on the jumbo screen as they prepare the field for their upcoming game. The commentator points out how the umpire has marked the ball. Everyone is on the edge of their seats in anticipation of the pitch. Once again, the pitch blazes toward the plate. I trust in the ease of my swing and again make perfect contact. This time, the ball is climbing higher than ever. In fact, it is still rising as it exits the stadium! Disbelief reigns again. The press box gets a phone call—it's from the grounds crew in Los Angeles. They said the ball just landed on their field. Sure enough, it has a red "X" on it. The umpire is called over to a monitor and confirms the marking is the exact one that he put on the ball.

No one knows how this could possibly happen. Did the ball get caught in the airstream? Did it enter a black hole? No one can explain it. It is magical, yet it is reality. Miracles do happen. Just because we don't know how they happen, doesn't keep them from happening. With each at-bat representing a major success in my life, I tell myself,
"I AM ROCKIN' THIS WHOLE LIFE!"

I have since created a shortened version of the visualization where I simply recall that feeling of hitting the ball. The rest of the feeling comes trailing along now that I have this image implanted in my head.

The Magic Begins

Within a few months of starting my feel-good techniques, an opportunity came to me out of the blue to invest in a promising start-up company. A few days later, on my birthday, the CEO of the company called to discuss the details. This company had a new product that would change an entire industry. This was not one of those too-good-to-be-true types of stories. I am trained in investments and could recognize the potential, as well as the risks. "What a birthday gift!" I thought to myself, as I contemplated placing a large percent of my net worth into the investment.

First, though, I wanted to see if Holly and the Elders could shed any light on this opportunity. This reading confirms many Universal truths and proves that practicing specific vibrations and visualizations really works.

Holly Burns—Reading

The first thing the Elders want to say is they want you to be aware that you brought this opportunity to yourself by working with your consciousness. You need to be congratulated, because everything is really rolling in the right direction as a result of your decisions. You are the one that made it all happen, including but not limited to this opportunity.

They want to go back to where you were when we did our phone reading a while back. You could have gone completely downhill, but instead you became more aware of how to be a deliberate creator. You have been following the path that you're being led to, or in other words, the path of least resistance.

They want you to recognize things for what frequency they came from. They are saying to you, "Did this investment opportunity come from good thoughts and a good frequency, or did it come from a lower or bad frequency?"

They also want you to think about what you've been asking the Universe for that matches this opportunity—for example, retiring young, getting rich quickly, taking adventures, living in the fast lane of manifestation, etc. I am just making those up, but you get the picture. When you recognize why things come into your reality, you will be more confident of the choices you make regarding them. They want you to first and foremost see if you can identify where this came from. Is it from something negative that you perpetually worry about, or is it a match from something more positive? I think it's something good.

You get the point: you've made great progress with your thoughts, and all positive things that have happened to you recently reflect that.

Ah… they just told me what it's a match for. You want to do something that makes you experience the vibration of the magician, the most in-it-to-win-it, charismatic guy in my tarot card deck. The magician is like the dude at the casino that everyone crowds around to watch how he handles a high stakes game of whatever he's playing. He's like that dude in those beer ads when he says, "I'm the most interesting man in the world." You were asking the Universe for experiences in this one frequency where you get to experience something that makes you feel like you TOTALLY KILLED IT and you could feel like you're getting a taste of the ultimate.

They are now asking you if you feel compelled to make the investment. Do you feel it calling to you? Does it feel like between this and anything else you could be investing in right now, this has the brightest light beaming over it? The Universe is showing you the path to take, and you can feel it calling you. When that happens, it means you are in your flow, and the Universe is saying, "Okay, do this! This rocks!"

They're saying that you want them to tell you the future—whether it will be great or not: what the outcome will be before you do it. You only need to know how you feel about it. Is the path before you totally lit up? They want you to trust this first and foremost. You will go away from the reading with more skills and will more deeply understand this one concept, which I will now explain further.

They want you to feel for that path and trust it. They want you to be happy with just knowing each day what you feel you should be doing. Everything could change tomorrow, but this day you are sure of your choices and you don't look back. This keeps you tuned in to the most direct path to success. Living like this, without needing any specific outcomes ahead of time, keeps you in the highest state of consciousness. This, in turn, brings you the coolest, most awesome physical manifestations.

They are pretty much putting in bold print what you already know you feel, so that should give you the confidence you need to make your decision about whether to invest or not. You have been feeling like the magician a lot lately, and this is the match for that.

You have brought yourself something super cool from your vibrational vortex that could possibly give you everything you ever wanted. We people never think something like this could drop in our laps but look what just popped up for you. If you let the Universe bring you its abundance, it will present itself to you in mysterious ways that you would never think of on your own. The Universe is way smarter than we are! It's like you tuned yourself to the vibration of, "I'm going to ROCK THIS WHOLE LIFE!" and this is what you are getting back.

"I'm going to rock this whole life!" and "I totally killed it." Holly tapped into two word-for-word sayings that I had been telling myself. I hadn't uttered those words to a single Soul.

The funny thing is, after I had been practicing this vision for a while, I noticed a picture hanging in a back room of our office at work. It's a painting of what appears to be Babe Ruth swinging the bat at Yankee Stadium with the ball sailing away from him. The Universe acknowledged my efforts with that picture, and then, Holly tapped into the same thing.

As you might have guessed, I left this reading feeling very empowered with much verification that these tools really work. First, I received direct confirmation that the Universe was hearing my thoughts. Second, I had manifested a great investment opportunity. Third, I knew that consciousness plays in the realm of feelings, vibrations, and visualizations, and that really, really works! From here on out, I was in control of my destiny. Fourth, I confirmed that we are not alone. We are being assisted by a team of Spirit Guides that want to help us and teach us in any way possible. Fifth, and perhaps most importantly, I was happy and was not turning back. I knew the "rules" and had practice working with them. Now, life would be fun as I tried to fine-tune my play at this "game." The other fun aspect about this process is seeing what the Universe will manifest to match your feeling. It is like Christmas morning over and over again.

This really is an incredible world we live in. I can't help but think back on my prior perspective of trying to please the outside world through work and effort with few signs of success. What a difference living life with the right concepts makes, knowing we are loved and fully supported.

Maybe living in this manner comes naturally to some people; perhaps they witnessed their parents living like this. As I watch highly successful people, I observe the air of confidence they carry with them. Sadly, for many of us, this is unnatural. Reacting to the outside world when "life hits you in the head with a brick" seems more common. Who knew we could pivot our focus, or better yet, avoid the brick being thrown in the first place, by living in a positive stream of thoughts and feelings? I do think some bricks were planned during our pre-birth planning phase, but only with the intent to pave our way to new heights. Using my life as an example, I would not be allowing my current successes if I hadn't first encountered my own share of bricks. Once again, don't be premature to judge people or situations. It's all good and in the flow.

The final piece of evidence that "feeling from the end" really works is this book in your hands. As a first-time author, many overwhelming thoughts can plant seeds of doubt in one's head. Finding reasons to quit would have been easy. Redirecting our focus from fear to the feeling of success is the secret that takes us from just dreaming to actually achieving our dreams.

Two things prevented these fears from taking control: remaining a clear vessel for God to work through and the feeling of this completed book in my hands. The image of this book sat in my hands on many chairlift rides while skiing in Utah. I could feel the smooth, glossy cover, see the book on shelves in bookstores, smell the fresh paper as I opened boxes of new shipments. These images kept my doubts at bay. My only job was to sit back and watch how this reality would unfold. That is the excitement of life, my friends.

Affirmations

Things are always working out for me.

I enjoy my thoughts so much, it doesn't even matter if they materialize.

Today, I release all limitations and am open to what the Universe will provide.

All my restrictions are melting away.

What if I dropped all restrictions and expectations just for this moment?

I allow miracles easily and effortlessly.

Outrageous joy is the product of my powerful thinking.

It was easy. It was fun. It was miraculous. It is done.

The things on their way to me are so much better than the things I could plan.

Everything works out for me in the most marvelous and unexpected ways.

I am excited to see how the Universe will fill my request.

I can have it all. I can have it now.

What if I allowed something more quickly?

I am the magician!

I totally killed it!

I am rockin' this whole life!

GOING WITH THE FLOW

Those who flow as life flows, know they need no other source.

~Lao Tzu*

This entire book is about going with the flow of life and following your intuition. However, "going with the flow" warrants a little more explanation. Let's dive in.

Aruba Story

One particular experience provided me with a better explanation of "going with the flow." I was on the longest vacation of my life—two weeks in Aruba! My significant other had found cheap airline tickets and a free home exchange, so it was a very inexpensive vacation, to boot! While there, we got into a very healthy routine. Each morning, we started with yoga, breakfast with a cup of homemade espresso, a workout by the pool, and some good reading/meditation. The afternoon would be spent scuba diving or exploring in a topless jeep. Evenings consisted of grilling seafood by the pool with a glass of wine. I had never been in a better state of mind. Stress had completely melted away. Physically, I was also feeling extremely vibrant and healthy. I highly recommend taking at least a two-week vacation to anyone who can. It will help immensely with getting into the flow of the Universe.

On the morning of our return trip, we made one last stop to the northern tip of the island. Strong waves, pushed by the east trade winds, cascaded upon the shore. Meditating and reflecting on the wonderful trip, I moved slowly about the rocky shore. There was a serenity to my consciousness. Thoughts had largely subsided, and I was feeling a deep sense of clarity and awareness.

A message started being relayed to me. The message was about how these waves have been crashing into these shores since the beginning of time. They escorted explorers here hundreds of years ago and have been consistently arriving without fail—rhythmically coming, wave-after-wave, year-after-year.

The abundance of the Universe is much the same, the message stated. It is always flowing to us unconditionally. It is only a matter of how much of this abundance we allow to flow into our lives. Abundance is our birthright—abundance of health, abundance of wealth, abundance of joy—you name it. You don't have to earn it. Just get out of the way and allow it. Surrender...Allow...Trust. Trust so much that it becomes knowing.

I am finally understanding that it is about ease.   ~Unknown

The message also left me with the gift of a meditation. I use this highly effective tool perhaps more than anything else in my toolbox.

Meditation

I picture myself on a warm, sunny, sandy ocean beach.
I am lying on my back in the water at the edge of a gently sloping shore.
My back is lightly touching the sand as the water partially supports me.
The sand is so polished that it feels silky to the touch.
My eyes are lightly closed, but the warm light filters through my eyelids.
The water has left a subtle, salty taste on my lips.
Gentle waves roll in from my right side.
Inhaling deeply, I say the word "relax" as my lungs fill to capacity.
The air in my lungs lifts me gently off the sand.
I feel the weightlessness as I pause my breathing.
Exhaling, I say the word "allow" as a wave pushes me gently down the beach.
At the end of my exhale, my bottom and shoulder blades sink down
and are again lightly supported by the sand.
I repeat these inhales and exhales, letting the tide take me
exactly where I need to go.
I feel the ease and lightness in my body throughout the process.
This is the feeling of allowing all abundance.
No restrictions, no resistance.
Trust the waves. Ease is the way.
Relaxing, I get exactly where I'm supposed to be.
Surrendering, allowing, trusting.
I am in the flow.

Once you get used to the feeling described in the meditation, you can repeat the words "relax" and "allow" in rhythm with your breathing to get you back to that place of allowing.

As I left the beach, I asked it for permission to take a memento of our experience. I chose a piece of dead coral rock that was bleached white, with porous holes throughout. The slight lengthwise curve fit nicely in the palm of my hand. Periodically, I hold the rock above my head and shower myself with the same abundance that I felt that final day in Aruba.

First, know that there is a flow, and it is always present. We can choose to allow it or resist it. Second, know that there are no hindrances to this flow that are not self-imposed.

Do not struggle. Go with the flow of things, and you will find yourself at one with the mysterious unity of the Universe.

~Chuang Tzu*

Now that we know there is a flow, let's briefly reiterate the process of navigating the flow. It has been said that in Zen there are only two things: sitting and sweeping the garden. Being in the flow begins with sitting, or the clearing phase. Finding stillness allows us to go from a negative momentum state to a neutral state by eliminating noisy, negative thoughts and emotions.

Moving from negative momentum to neutral is, by definition, positive momentum. This positive momentum will not stop at neutral. The spaciousness in the neutral state acts like a vacuum, and the positive momentum brings forth inspired ideas and action. Learning to find mental stillness allows this flow. That's why the title of this book is *Clear Vessels*. Become clear so abundance and creativity can flow to you. It is very straightforward in the beginning, but then, we can play with the subtle, higher vibrations.

As the positive momentum brings forth ideas, spend time downloading or soaking in these ideas. These are the ideas to act on. Pick the ones that feel the best, jump in, and don't look back. When all this downloading and inspired action starts to feel like work, it is time to sit again.

If what you are doing doesn't feel good, you are either doing the wrong thing or you are doing it in the wrong way.

~The Elders

How big can you dream without doubt or reason stepping in? This is the answer to how much good you will allow in your life. Can you get comfortable with the thought of a faster, bigger flow of abundance? I challenge myself to think bigger, better, more clearly, and more often…and to know when to just be. That is my definition of going with the flow. This is my discipline and play.

Being in the flow is the ultimate goal. This is about the present, where all power, creation, and allowing resides, and it allows for a more enjoyable journey. Anything that happens as a result of being in the flow is just icing on the cake. This attitude of non-attachment to whatever is or whatever comes is the perfect place of allowing and flowing.

Here's another real-world example of how I play with this. Sometimes, when it is convenient and I feel compelled, I buy a lottery ticket. I think about how I would use that money, the trips I would take, the houses I would buy, and the people I would help. I let these feelings spiral to wherever they want to go and enjoy feeling my way through that. And that is why one wants the money: to feel good, right? Well, if I already feel good, I don't need the money anymore. That is when the money can come, directly or indirectly.

One's ships come in over a calm sea.
~Florence Scovel Shinn

Maybe you are not entirely sold on that premise, but as you become accomplished at making yourself feel consistently good, nothing else matters. Whatever is meant for me will come for me at the perfect time. Until then, I will keep enjoying each moment and each day. It's kind of exciting, knowing that this is the ideal environment for miracles to appear. Using the gardening analogy, this is the fertile ground of your Soul. As I like to tell myself:

It has to come easy, because it can't come hard.

How much ease can you sink yourself into? That is really the challenge.

Native American culture has long understood the principles of flow. Some tribes have a tradition called the "Giveaway Ceremony" or the "Potlatch." While the ceremony can take various forms, it generally involves tribal members setting meaningful possessions on a blanket, and selecting items from others to keep as a gift. This offering of gratitude keeps the energy flowing. In more extreme variations, members give away all their possessions. This allows for personal growth through a form of non-attachment. This is also a display of trust. The one gifting understands that he does not need the material goods, as Great Spirit or other tribal members will provide what is needed, when it is needed. No one will be abandoned. Everyone is cared for.

Our process of breathing is very similar. Do you fear the exhaling of air from your lungs because you're not sure if there is any more to breathe? No, of course not! You always know that more air will be available when it is needed. Consciously pay attention to this now and notice the ease and trust of your most critical necessity.

I'll share one last visualization. I imagine myself floating downstream in a kayak. I can choose to force my way around rocks, battle the current at turns, and worry about crashing into the shore. Or, I can let the river take me where it wants, glide me around obstacles, and take me to the perfect destination. You may have heard the expression "put the paddle down?" I say, "Hell, throw the paddle in the river!" I don't need it. Sure, I might hit some bumps or get a little water splashed on me, but when I arrive at my destination, those obstacles made the trip that much more enjoyable. Trust the flow, enjoy the journey, and whatever you do, don't paddle upstream! If we remain aware, our feelings will tell us when we are fighting the flow.

Reading

In this reading, we learn more about the path of least resistance, non-attachment, and trust.

Here is the background for the reading: I had two job opportunities pop up from previous employers and thought they were both worth considering. At times, my current job was insane, but I learned to work within those confines and be happy despite the circumstances. The two years I spent there allowed plenty of time to fine-tune my vibrations. Life kept getting better and better, and it really didn't matter what came next. I had a hunch that my time there had served me well, but perhaps I was ready for a different phase in my life. Working for a past employer had the feeling of going backward in life and did not feel quite right.

Here is what Holly and the Elders had to say:

Until something feels great, no action is necessary. They are saying don't take either of the jobs unless you are excited about the changes. Know those other jobs don't feel like moving toward freedom. Your path of least resistance is no job, but you have thrown resistance on that path, as we all do.

Pay attention to your dreams and your intuition; you are hearing your Soul speak to you. They are calling you to live in touch with the deeper parts of your consciousness. They also suggest meditating for a closer relationship with them. Just keep noticing all the little things. They talk to you all day long; just notice it. Work more on that level where things just jump out to you. Trust that more. That is us!

There is a voice that doesn't use words. Listen.

~Rumi*

You will get whatever you are lined up with as far as the freedom from having to work goes. What you are ready to allow to happen to yourself is what will come. We all could win the lottery tomorrow or have a lot of other things happen to us that would allow us to be wealthy for the rest of our lives, but we disallow most of it from interacting with us.

They want me to share this story with you: I was watching a video on YouTube of a woman who is a professional psychic, life coach, and public speaker/motivator. She said, "I decided I could allow myself to get paid just for being me, and the next day a check for six figures showed up in the mail." It might not have been the next day, but it was damn soon after she decided that.

They are saying, "It's as easy to create a castle as it is a button." You have some rigidity in your allowing when it comes to letting yourself get to where you don't need to work. You think there are "acceptable" ways to do it, and you want it to happen in one of those ways, mostly to prove that your career was worthwhile. You don't want to think that you're not good enough at your investment job, so to get rich overnight would not be allowed for you. It's all just stupid stuff! Drop all the stupid stuff and jump off the cliff without a parachute and let more abundance in!

The Elders just added, "You have the power within yourself to accomplish anything you wish."

It also helps to try on other people's paces. Think about how much abundance people like Justin Bieber, Selena Gomez, Kylie Jenner, and Taylor Swift allowed in very short amounts of time. They couldn't have had any guilt issues, or it would not have happened. It goes down to a very subtle level— how much we allow to come in, at what pace, and from where.

Work on just letting that go. Just put in what it is that you want. You don't have to get specific, just put in "I don't want to have to work anymore" or "I want to have enough money to do whatever I want." Know the difference between really aligning with that trajectory and just putting a toe in. Some of your limiting beliefs are causing you to not fully step onto it.

They said, "Well, of course, you already know that, because if you had, you'd be super rich and not have to work right now, and we wouldn't be having this conversation."

I know I could have been super rich earlier in my life. I could have done it yesterday, but I am okay with the pace I'm on, and I don't feel any ill will toward people who kick my ass in that area. I just understand they don't have any resistance toward letting it in, and I have a little bit to work on. I am very happy with where I'm going, how I'm getting there, and how things have come about for me. That's where you must be, and I can feel you are very close to that in all aspects.

You are at a crossroads and have no idea where each road will end. Pick one that strikes your fancy and set out with courage and a light heart. Prepare to meet all challenges with confidence. Regarding unconventional choices, the Elders are telling you to "take a leap of faith."

They want you to work more on learning about when you're in or out of your flow, as well, but that's another huge thing. First, they want you to test your relationship with your inner being throughout the day. When something big comes along, you will have established a good enough relationship to fully trust the answer.

They are saying, "Let's test that right now on something big. What do you think your inner being is telling you about those other job offers?" I am guessing you would say, "My inner being is saying I don't need to take any of them, and the jobs aren't really what I want, so I should pass." Keep on testing yourself all day long on everything you are wondering about, and then when the outcome comes, you can see if you were right or not.

This is all a super fine-tuned thing. Recognizing when you are in the flow is the first step. Knowing how to get back into it is the second. Or sustaining it,

that is the better second step. This is about always following your path
of least resistance, period.

I live like this all the time. I always do what calls to me the loudest when I
get up every day. I might go to bed with the whole day planned out, and then
I wake up and something else jumps ahead of my plans and calls to me more
loudly. I always do what calls to me and dump my other plans. That never
fails me. I am always so glad that I trusted my flow
to know the right thing to do.

This also helps with decision making. Ask your inner being what feels
aligned, what feels in the flow, and do that one.
ALWAYS.
Always, always, always.

There are so many lessons in these readings that are self-evident. The big takeaway is to observe how even the smallest thought vibrations can impact reality. Personally, I view this information to be fun, challenging, empowering, and at a different level than anything I ever encountered. At some point, I realized I had to share this information with the world. I am forever grateful for Holly and the Elders.

Affirmations

Abundance flows effortlessly to me in the most unexpected ways.

My positive flow allows all good things to come to me.

The flow is my goal, not the manifestation.

I just have fun and the Universe takes care of all the details.

I am always aware of my signs and love following their leads.

I never miss the opportunities that rain down upon me. I catch them all!

*I am very happy where I am, I'm happy with my pace,
and I'm excited about the future.*

Things come easily to me because they can't come hard.

The price I have to pay is ease, not effort.

I am comfortable with a faster flow of abundance.

My dominant intent is to feel joy.

I am playful and courageous in my pursuit of joy.

In any moment, anything is possible.

The Universe is conspiring to give me everything I want.

What the Universe has done for others, it now does for me.

What if I allowed the Universe to amaze me today?

FINE-TUNING OUR VIBRATIONS

True alignment and true happiness come from within you and radiate out.

~The Elders

So far, we have discussed clearing, allowing, and visualizing. This chapter emphasizes the final steps of the process—trusting and knowing. This pertains not only to the objects of our desires, but also to the grand plans of our lives. Most of this chapter is from Holly and the Elders, with my comments interspersed.

One thing was bothering me when I requested this reading. Earlier, the Elders said my investment opportunity would generate wealth rather soon, and the next time they said it might take up to ten years. I did not want to be disrespectful, but fair is fair, so I asked Holly if I had somehow changed the timeline with a change in my thinking. They also said I had missed out on opportunities for abundance that they had been sending my way. Not wanting to miss out, I thought some insight on improving my receptiveness would be helpful. Here's how the reading went:

That question about changing the timeline was awesome! I was just doing some learning on all that myself. The Elders are saying that all your questions are very good! Because you are digging deeper with your thinking, they want to explain that it's not about those questions. Instead, it's about a deeper level of KNOWING. That is precisely what you have been asking to do better, so you are totally on the right track here.

I love how the Elders know exactly who they are talking to. Personally, I don't want answers that dance around the topic

—just tell it to me straight. On the other hand, I can be easily discouraged. I had to laugh when they said that my questions were very good, but "it's not about those questions." That was a perfect response for me.

They are saying your questions are taking you to a deeper level, which then will eliminate a lot of these questions. It's about feeling the underlying energy of the flow, not necessarily determining if the facts are correct or incorrect. It's about being in touch with your flow and feeling for that. The reason behind the current situation is often beyond our scope to know in the moment. We really can't accurately assess as it's happening whether a situation is good or bad, correct or incorrect, etc.

Let me clarify: In life, it is easy to get caught up thinking that physical action is the solution. But really, what surrounds you is a reflection of your emotions and thoughts. The Elders are asking you to take a step back from your physical reality and look at the Earth from 30,000 feet in the sky. Things seem so different from here, don't they? You can encompass millions of people's lives at once, and all the little details merge to become one overall idea. That is what they want you to look for in your life, that larger overall plan. Feel for that.

They are asking you to see the physical plane like that, to remove yourself from where you are entrenched, with your focus on the physical surroundings and physical events. Start to focus more on the flow and feel for that underlying energy that is present in everything you do. For instance, you see someone smiling at you, but you can tell they are really feeling intense emotional pain. Which aspect of that experience are you going to put the most focus on, the physical smile or the energy behind it?

Here's another example. You want to go to the beach today, but the forecast says there's a 40% chance of rain. How do you feel about that? Do you think you're going to be able to go and have a great time, or do you feel something else redirecting your choice of activity?

*Let's say you choose to switch activities and then at about 4 PM
you find out why: it's pouring rain at the beach.*

*Or, do you go to the beach and end up getting rained on? If you feel like you
should go, you should go no matter what, because the flow says to go and
that's the best result possible for you. So, you get there and it's pouring rain.
You end up stuck in the car with your friend waiting for the rain to subside
and end up having a once-in-a-lifetime discussion. That is living from that
underlying current of flow that always pulls you toward the best path for you.*

*Now to your questions about missed abundance opportunities and if the
investment is really going to take ten years to come to fruition. You know that
it felt aligned when you made the investment. You are no longer getting in
the way of what the Universe wants to bring and are letting the Universe do
the driving for you. You are living each moment of your life in the flow, and
whatever the flow has in store for you is the best thing. So, you know that the
timing of that investment will work out for you in the best possible way,
no matter what specific events occur.*

*Knowing to follow your flow, you begin to approach your decisions from
an entirely different perspective. You used to think like this: "I made this
investment and if it doesn't pay off, I will deem it a failure and a bad
decision." Now, you are living on this frequency: "I am excited for today.
I am feeling such good energy coming my way. I feel a huge buildup of good
things coming my way right now. I can feel huge abundance that I have been
working to manifest, and I can feel it is really going to start showing up in the
physical for me in a huge way, very soon. I know it's right there.
I have no idea what it is; I just know it's there!"*

*And you begin to recognize things differently. When, what, where, and how it
will play out still fascinates you, and you wonder if you are shifting timelines,
but you wonder with this underlying peace in your heart. You know it felt
right the day you put your money in. Nothing else matters. The outcome is
really the Universe's job. You did your part and put your money in as the
Universe directed you. If you trust that, then trust the rest
to play out for your highest good.*

119

The Elders said that even if you did shift timelines due to negative emotions, etc, you could still shift back with positive ones!

The Universe is always bringing you the highest possible flow that you will allow in every moment. You need not be overly concerned with when that investment shows back up in your pocket as money, because you can't do anything about it. The Universe knew what it was getting you into when it led you to the opportunity. We do not, much of the time, fully understand why we're led to certain things. Later, once all the dots are connected, we can see the hows and whys of what the Universe is orchestrating for us.

This is all about living from that perspective of your life, not from the physical specifics of it not happening yet. There is a frenzy of energetic activity taking place, and you can tap into that feeling if you want.
That is the answer to trust the most.

You might have put that money in so that you would manifest ten times more than that. You might have invested in that company because you were supposed to meet someone down the line that will have another investment that will pay off ten times more than this one. Whatever the reason, we know that the initial decision was in the flow, so trust that.

There are infinite ways for you to become so super-wealthy that you won't have to work anymore. Know that the Universe knows about them and wants to flow them to you. This is the deeper level of thinking and consciousness that they are asking you to shift to.

The way to become more at peace about all those things you want to happen is to get up to speed with your flow and see how that feels. When you are there, just trust the Universe's intelligence and your own inner being to lead you to what is best for you at all times.

Listening to this advice, I practiced the feeling of things coming to me more quickly. What would it be like if I put up no resistance, and everything came at a much faster pace? I made peace with the notion of "outrageous abundance." I asked, "What would it be like if I totally allowed whatever the Universe wanted to provide, even just for this day?"

After this reading as I drove down the highway, I imagined what it was like to be in these fast cars flying by me. I used this as a metaphor for allowing at a faster pace. Could I be comfortable at that pace? It's like when you first get on the interstate. You tend to drive a little slower than the pace of traffic at first, but after a few minutes, you are more comfortable with the high speeds and begin to drive faster. I had done a lot of creating in the unmanifested world; would I now be ready to receive these gifts at a faster pace? In other words, could I weed out all limiting thoughts, no matter how small they may be?

The techniques that the Elders are teaching in this reading are precisely the ones I used in the "Hunching" chapter as I planned my ski trip to Utah. Now you understand why it felt like I was being applauded every step of the way on that journey. The Universe was confirming that my efforts were working. They love to co-create with us.

Now, how do you get into your flow? You always take the path of least resistance. Live with as little resistance in your life as you can. Don't let things pile up and build into vortexes of negativity. Instead, jump into your flow by having that conversation with that person right away, or by letting go of all negative thinking about something, as opposed to dwelling on it for days. You always do what feels better.

If you have a choice between two things and you can't pick, feel for the right choice. Which one would feel better when it is all done? Which one would be the easiest to transition to? Feel for the one your heart says it wants to do more and don't dwell on your choices once you made them. Get in and don't think as much. The human mind wants to second-guess things. Decide in the moment, and then put it in the done folder so you can keep your thoughts up to speed with what the flow is dishing out to you.

They are now giving me a way for you to get more clarity on how to allow the abundance they are raining down on you. Don't worry about the specific steps if you don't know any. Just get in the flow and stay there. The flow will then lead you right to them. When you are lost, get in the flow, and don't worry about the exact steps to take.

Now here's the tricky part: How do you know if you are in the flow or not? That is what they are teaching you right now. You've got to feel your way through it.

Living life on your highest frequency is always the goal. This will always lead you to perfect timing, so there's no need to second-guess yourself.

Here's an example: Today, I was sitting at a family event wondering when to start motorcycling for home so that I could avoid the approaching rain clouds. For some reason, I didn't feel compelled to leave at that time. Instead, it felt like I should wait a short while, so I did. Then a short while later, I suddenly felt an overwhelming urge to leave. I knew that was the time to make a dash for it. I rode right between a couple of huge storm clouds, but none hit me.

Never violate a hunch.

~Florence Scovel Shinn

Halfway home, I saw a humongous cloud headed my way. I was faced with the decision to wait until it passed, keep riding toward it, or reroute to the west. Rerouting would be about a 35-minute detour, but it would bring me in behind that storm.

Continuing on the current route felt the most flowy. It didn't feel flowy to get home later. Also, I decided not to hold on to the idea that I must get home in a certain fashion or at a certain time; rather, I stayed open to solutions from

the Universe with no limiting thoughts from myself.
I thought, "Okay, fine, I'll chance it. If I must stop under an overpass for a half-hour, so be it." I could feel my inner being say, "You'll make it home just fine this way." And I did. I rode right between two huge clouds and was home no less than five minutes when it started to rain. The rain kept up for over an hour. I'm sure you have many stories like that, too.

Recognize when you're in your flow on autopilot, so you can purposely keep yourself there the rest of the time, too.

Let's revisit your exact questions now that they have gotten that huge, huge concept across to you sparked by your initial questions:

Regarding whether the timing of your investment has changed, they are explaining another dimension to their answers. Multiple things can be in the works all stemming from that original investment. Part of it can be almost done and another part might come to fruition over the long run. There has been no shift from the original timeline, but many other "fissures" are manifesting as a result of those past choices. That is the flow right there. We don't always know why we are doing things, but afterward we can see it if we know what to look for.

I have often done things that did not prove fruitful directly, but they put my mind on a specific frequency long enough to manifest something else from it. It's always for my best, even if it didn't work out in the way I thought it was going to initially. Looking back, I can see why the Elders have told me to do things—not because it was going to directly work out, but for more intricate reasons that I had no awareness of at the time.

All I can do at any moment is trust the feeling of that moment. Yes or no? I test it, and then I act based on what I felt at that moment. It's a simple formula.

They are saying your questions will shift if you see your life from this perspective and live it from this perspective. You won't be concerned about making the right decisions anymore, because you will see all your choices, no matter what the outcomes, as good ones. You made them from within your flow, and the flow never steers us wrong!

No matter the timeline on that investment, or the outcome, what you do with your time puts you into a trajectory. You started to think thoughts of being a millionaire; you began to feel more abundant just from knowing that someday it's going to pay off for you. You started spending that money in your head. The Elders just said, "Well worth it!"

They want you to try an experiment. Try living as if you have a blindfold on to anything going on in the physical plane. Practice feeling your way around and not getting too caught up in what exact things are going on. They want to teach you to feel your flow more clearly and to trust it deeper. This will speed up the momentum of everything around you, so be ready for it! You will no longer slow things down by spending time creating your own resistance.

The non-physical, and what you feel from it, will tell you a whole hell of a lot more than the physical plane ever will. Try it for a while; focus more on the non-physical information you receive telepathically than the specifics of the physical plane. I would love to get a report back from you about how this goes for you!

Here's an example to better explain what they are talking about: Something comes along in your life, and you feel something about it. You can trust that explicitly, or you can react to the physical plane's stimuli. If they are in conflict, you can easily get confused and lose your way. If you trust the Universe's infinite intelligence and your flow, circumstances on the physical plane don't confuse you, even if they seem to totally conflict with the energetic level. You will know they don't, and the two will come together at the right time.

They want you to start doing some experimentation with that. For instance, Joel Osteen just told this story: A man came to one of his gatherings and felt compelled to go over and give this woman he didn't know what cash he had.

He only had $5 on him. He kept thinking, "How dumb is that to walk up to a stranger and hand her only five dollars?" But he did it. And the woman said, "Oh my gosh, thank you so much! I don't have enough gas to get home, but God told me to come anyway, so I did. I had no idea how I was going to get home afterward!" That man was able to ignore all the physical actions happening around him and act on what the flow told him to do. The same could be said for the lady.

Now the Elders want to talk about the abundances they have rained down upon you that you did not receive. You are exposed to things that initially get you excited, but then snuff out the excitement with practicalities or other excuses. Or you forget about them. They are talking about the energy going back and forth, but not getting anywhere. That is you stopping the higher vibrating ideas from coming after the initial exposure.

I call that "reaching for the high-vibrating idea." Use these catapulting experiences more to your advantage. Either run with the initial idea or, if you don't want to take it literally, use the original thought as a catalyst to something you like even more. Let your mind soar around that frequency long enough to download ideas. You have been provided ideas that may not have been direct abundance opportunities, but they were close enough for you to connect to some downloads.

The Elders are saying you are doing nothing wrong; you are progressing super well on your journey to a higher consciousness. Don't beat yourself up, because you are doing it perfectly for you. When you are fully ready to not have to work anymore, something will shift in you.

Don't worry about all that now; live in the flow. The answers should come from there, not from "efforting" them into place by overthinking. That's your own human mind trying to figure it out and getting in the way. Let the Universal impulses lead you along to your own personal creek with the perfect flow for you. The flow works totally differently from the human mind. The human mind wants to plan it all out first, and only then go live it. The Universe wants to not tell you a damned thing ahead of time and only give you the next little tiny step. It expects you to just take these steps, unconditionally and without question. The two must be dealt with and brought into balance. This goes for every human.

Search for what makes you feel good. Act from your place of inner passion for something. Don't think so hard. Instead, just follow where your feelings seem to be leading you, and don't question it or think it over too much.

The Elders will not reveal any more specifics on the whereabouts of the abundance opportunities. Get into your flow and find them organically, not from them telling you. So, that's pretty much your assignment: see what your flow tells you.

Well, that was a massive dose of information, don't you think? These readings teach us that our most subtle thoughts impact our realities. It also shows that it is only natural for us to vary in our clarity. One day, we might be in a perfect allowing mode, and the next day we might be throwing in some resistance. That's okay but become aware of the difference. The awareness allows us to massage our feelings by consciously directing our focus. We never stop creating, whether we are aware of it or not, so we might as well be creating intentionally and effectively. This is where life gets fun. It's like trying to master the highest level of a video game. Hopefully, you were able to soak up the lessons, even if they were rooted in the specifics of my situation. Thank you, Elders!

Meditation

I breathe into my heart and feel the energy expand throughout my body.

I repeat several breaths.

I notice the tingling of my entire body.

I expand my focus to notice the sensations on my skin.

As I do this, the energy now surrounds the exterior of my body.

My physical body fades into a ball of pure energy.

With each breath into my heart, my energy field grows larger and larger.

My energy now encompasses my house. Then my town. The entire country.

The Earth.

As it grows, I become clearer and stronger.

Now I encompass the entire galaxy.

My rays of energy shoot out into the Universe at great speed.

There is no end to me.

Sitting here in space, I notice my vastness, my presence, and my power.

Bringing my focus back, I concentrate my attention on my inner core

of intense energy, about ten feet in diameter, floating in space.

As I do this, I am approached by another extremely bright ball of white light,

about three times the size of mine.

I sense an immense peace and power. It is overwhelming love. It is God.

I am invited in, and my energy field merges

into this warm, peaceful, loving light.

My energy is magnified, much like when the flames of two candles touch.

My body has never felt the intensity of this love.

As I look around in this sphere of energy, I can no longer tell where

I end and God begins.

Our energy is the same. We are one.

Looking down at planet Earth from way above, I see a thunderstorm

and note a tiny flash of lightning.

Funny, on Earth that is an extreme form of power.

But now, I realize that I am so much more powerful by comparison.

I have the power to create worlds.

By simply directing my focus, I can go anywhere, do anything,

and create anything.

I know what it means to be made in the image of God.

MAGICAL PART OF YOU

Stop acting so small. You are the Universe in ecstatic motion.

~Rumi*

We are not who we think we are, and we are not doing what we think we are doing. We are part of something bigger. It's not all about us as individuals.

The identities we assume are just roles, and we strengthen these identities as we move through life. We harden our beliefs with repetitive thoughts about the world around us. These identities are now busy striving, working, attaining, competing against, and conquering the world and other people. The more we fight, the stronger the grasp this identity has on us, and the greater the mirage of the outside world becomes. Eventually, a crisis, or perhaps death, occurs, which releases our attachments to these identities. How long are we going to struggle before we get to this breaking point? Or, perhaps, we are lucky enough to have a crack of light open our eyes before the need for a crisis.

Who are we, and what are we doing?

We are pure consciousness, a consciousness with access to immense creative power and wisdom. This power is harnessed through our clarity and focus.

This is a truth that has been known for thousands of years. Why this truth is kept under wraps and why we are fed false limitations and fictitious rules is beyond me. Jesus came to awaken us to this truth, yet two thousand years later, many of us are still asleep.

I was blind but now I see!

Know that not only can we create our own worlds, but we are creating them. Don't like what you see? Change it. We can live joy-filled lives; we can be, do, or have whatever we want. The choice is ours, and we are making this choice in every moment. When we choose fearlessly and intentionally, the only limitations are in our heads. Or, we can continue to live blindly, focusing on the external world, which is nothing but a deceitful image, a mere reflection of our ingrained beliefs and fears. We may not have known the error of our ways before. Now, we have the knowledge. And now, we can choose to live.

Truly, the greatest gift you have to give is that of your own self-transformation.

~Lao Tzu

We do not have to take these steps alone. In fact, we are never alone. I know it can be scary. At times, we are like toddlers in a swimming pool for the first time with our moms. We must learn how to operate in this new environment. We have to trust that we are fully supported. We cannot drown; we can only thrive and enjoy ourselves. Eventually, we will be splashing and having fun. First, take a step, each and every day of your life going forward. All we have to figure out is which step feels the best today. And since the best next step is always the one that feels the best, what is holding you back?

Here's a tip on how to get started: the first step is to just be. Be you. We are beautiful, loving, wonderful, powerful beings made in the image of God. We are conscious vortices of love, and love is the most powerful energy in the Universe. We don't have to do a damn thing. We are enough—just the way we are.

When was the last time you were just you? The silent, all-knowing, all-loving, all-encompassing Soul that you are? Just be right now. Mentally surround yourself with warm, white, radiant light. Feel the energy in your heart, and now throughout your body. Drop all roles, thoughts, and fears just for this minute. Will you allow yourself to do that? Ask yourself, if you must.

Now feel the sense of calm. Bathe in that security for just a bit. In the future, when you get lost in visions of the outside world, you can always return to your center of being. You are always safe.

We could stop right here. Implementing a practice of meditation into our lives to help us just "be" has been shown to produce great benefits. But this is a master's level class. We didn't come here to just get by. We came here to knock it out of the park.

As a drop in the ocean of consciousness, know that your separateness is nothing but an illusion. There is no one to compete with. What we do to others, we do to ourselves. We are all connected. We are all part of the infinite and all-knowing collective consciousness. As a card-carrying member of this club, we have full access to the collective wisdom and creative power of the Universe.

How do we access this power? You have already taken the first step. A minute ago, you became a clear vessel through which the creative forces of the Universe flow.

Now we can do one of two things with this flow: We can mold it by becoming a co-creator with the Universe, or we can pinch it off by falling back into old habits.

Our focus will undoubtedly lead us astray at times. That's alright. Our awareness allows us to quickly jump back into the flow. We are no longer attached to our thoughts; we are third-party observers. We pay attention to our feelings, which are the compass of our thoughts. And the great news is, we don't have to be perfect. Just being in the flow for short periods of time will result in dramatic improvements compared to where we once were. It is that powerful.

Many people are walking around in the dark, reacting to the outside world's stimulus with reptile-like reflexes, protecting an ego that they think is them. They don't even know that they have the power to direct their focus.

When we awaken, we become aware. We are aware of our thoughts but realize that we are not the thinkers. We are consciousness above the level of thought. We are aware of our emotions, and of how our thoughts impact our emotions. We observe all of this because we are none of this, and knowing that, we can simply be.

How will you navigate your day when you wake up tomorrow morning? Will you allow your monkey-mind to drive in a reactionary manner, or will you consciously seek clarity and create new habits of focus?

In this world of duality, for every good there is an evil. Which one are you going to focus on? That answer will tell you your future. Are you going to live a life of joy or a life of struggle? Are you going to swim with the current, or fight it? It is all up to us. Who will you choose to serve?

Lightening the mood for a minute, this reminds me of a joke I heard many years ago. A mother has young twin boys. One of them is never happy, no matter the circumstances, while the other is always happy. Trying to figure out this difference, the mother takes the boys to a psychiatrist. The doctor decides to run an experiment. He puts the unhappy boy in a closed room full of toys and the other boy in a room with a pile of horse manure.

Of course, the unhappy boy is in his room with the toys crying, while the happy boy is laughing and flinging dung all around. The doctor asks the first boy why he is crying. Well, the toys are the wrong ones, they don't work properly.

Then, the doctor talks to the happy boy. "Why are you so happy? We put you in a room with nothing but a pile of horse manure, yet you are having the time of your life."

The boy says, "With all of this horse poop, there has to be a pony in here somewhere!"

Life is going to give us what looks like a pile of poop some days. How will you respond? This is important. The time to plan a new habit is now, not in the moment. What will you do?

Let's start with what NOT to do. Our old selves may have gone here, but not your new version:

> *Don't complain.*
>
> *Don't speak negative words.*
>
> *Don't assume it will turn out like the past.*
>
> *Don't worry about figuring out all the details.*
>
> *Don't freak out.*
>
> *Don't blame someone else.*
>
> *Don't focus on what is not working.*
>
> *Insert any other old habit you have used here.*

Use your self-awareness to observe which of these things you have been using. *Don't judge; just observe.* Our awareness is now directing things. Awareness does not judge situations or people. It is not attached to outcomes, and it is not driven by ego. Awareness simply observes and heals.

Having observed unproductive patterns in our lives, let's now dig into our toolbox of be-happy tricks. We have tools for any situation—just pick the right tool for the job. With small jobs, multiple tools might work. Select the tool that feels right to you. Maybe you try one tool, and it doesn't work. Grab another one. The goal is to make yourself feel better.

We are all going to be bouncing up and down the emotional spectrum throughout our lives. Today's challenge will be different than tomorrow's. Our work is never done so long as we are breathing. One minute, we think we have life mastered; the next minute we are surprised by an emotional curveball. We never know when we'll need to pull out a tool that we thought we retired long ago. Below are some tools we've discussed that are now available to you:

Just being

Meditating to gain clarity

Listening to guided meditations

Practicing self-love

Forgiving our past

Navigating difficult conversations with awareness

Consciously deciding to be happy where we are

Pivoting our focus when faced with unpleasant obstacles

Practicing gratitude in mental or written format

Using positive affirmations to program our thoughts

Allowing nature to heal us and teach us

Keeping a journal of our thoughts, progress, affirmations, or dreams

Focusing on the "cups" that are filled up in our lives

Downloading solutions

Giving space for solutions to arise

Using our imagination to create intentional feelings

Looking to others as examples of success

Taking inspired action

Listening to the Universe/Spirit Guides

Looking for signs

Expecting good things to come

Following our bliss

Being playful in a serious situation

Trusting that the dots will connect

Hunching our way for the best-feeling option

Viewing situations from a desired solution

And when all else fails, giving it up to God

Holy smokes—look how talented you have become! Now go play with these tools as different situations arise. This is not work. This is the "Game of Life," and you have everything you need to succeed!

Create desired feelings, monitor the slightest twinges of thought, and then sit back and allow miracles to unfold before you. You are sitting on a mountain of gold but have been too preoccupied to notice.

You are now awake. See the beauty that surrounds you, as well as the beauty within. Have you ever really noticed how beautiful and how powerful you are? It brings tears to my eyes looking at all of this beauty without those old shades on.

Universal laws are all working for us, not against us. Vibrations really work. Isn't it amazing what a change in perception does? Every day is an opportunity to play in this magic kingdom. What are we going to do with it? Are you going to survive, skimp along, just get by . . . or are we going to knock it out of the park, rock this whole life, and create miracles? It's just as easy either way. And it is all up to you.

If you practice working with these tools and work with discipline to change your habits, the Universe will respond in perfect ways with amazing quickness and accuracy.

Each of us is love, and love is the most powerful thing in the Universe. And each of us is a gift, to ourselves and the world. Now that you know who you really are, it is time to live that expression and share it.

LETTER TO YOU

Sometimes as we go through the daily motions of life and don't realize how far we have come. Looking back on your progress can be inspiring and provide renewed confidence, courage, and hope for the future. You are quite amazing.

Let's take that exercise one step further by looking back from a future vantage point. Below is a letter that I wrote to myself from a place that I wanted to be. Write a letter to yourself. Where do you want to be? What does it feel like? What would you say to your current self?

Dear Me,
I am so proud of you!
You believed in the unbelievable.
You trusted the Universe.
You were coachable.
You fell in love with yourself.
You learned to be comfortable in any situation and in any conversation.
You have become the master of your destiny.
You are healing the wounds of your inner child.
You are no longer at the whims of other people.
You are your own creator.
You have remained humble and kind.
You are living the life that your Soul dreamed of.
You could have given up; you didn't.
You could have stumbled along; you didn't.
You decided to go big, and you did it!
You are complete and confident in every facet of your life.
I love you. I am proud of you. You are amazing.
Just thinking of how far you have come brings tears to my eyes.
Let's have fun and enjoy life like we never have before.
With all my loving awareness, Me

Affirmations

I am a gift to the world and myself.

My value to the planet is huge.

I am enough.

I ask for instructions and they are given, just like many other blessings in my life.

I have consciously decided that this is so.

I live in an abundant world.

Allowing abundance into my own life, I add to the world and to the lives of those I love.

My good energy feels so thick around me that manifestations must come.

Miracles appear every day.

I expect miracles!

What miracles can I allow today?

My desires are seeking me out.

It's going to be bigger than I thought, come quicker than I imagined, and be more rewarding than I dreamed.

All possibilities exist today.

As I show new vibrations, the Universe shows new miracles.

I have unlimited access to the power of the Universe.

I am always attracting my highest and most joyful path.

I am kind and I'm caring, I'm strong and I'm smart, I am loved and alive, I am fun and I'm friendly, I am peaceful and powerful, I am safe and secure.

I am comfortable with outrageous abundance.

I am ready to prosper beyond my wildest dreams.

My next chapter is going to be amazing!

This is the most exciting time of my life!

Life is so freaking cool, I can't stand it!

I am a clear vessel through which the God-force flows.

NOTES

Taking notes and writing down your thoughts will help you become a clear vessel.

_____

_____

_____

_____

_____

_____

_____

_____

_____

_____

_____

_____

_____

_____

_____

_____

APPENDIX

Quotes

* Quotes with an asterisk by the source were likely paraphrased over time with no direct original source document found. The message is still powerful, but likely has changed throughout time.

Bibliography

Holiday, Ryan. Ego is the Enemy. New York, NY: Penguin, 2016.

Joehle, Klaus. A Weekend With 'a' Drunken Leprechaun. Lincoln, NE: iUniverse, 2002.

Kribbe, Pamela. The Jeshua Channelings. United States: Booklocker.com, Inc, 2008.

Neville. The Power of Awareness. United States: Penguin, 2012. This edition also includes Awakened Imagination, first published in 1954. Power of Awareness was originally published in 1952.

Shinn, Florence Scovel. The Wisdom of Florence Scovel Shinn. New York, NY: Simon & Schuster, 1989. This is a compilation of four books by Florence Scovel Shinn—The Game of Life, The Power of the Spoken Word, Your Word Is Your Wand, and The Secret of Success.

ACKNOWLEDGMENTS

I want to recognize the efforts and talents of many people who helped this book become a reality.

Holly Burns provided the psychic talent and spiritual support that inspired this journey. She is a gift to the world! Heather Dakota saw my vision and was the missing link between an idea and a creation. She has the skills of an entire team and is a joy to know. Henry Cordes provided the editing, which made me appear smarter than I am. Michelle Richardson's photographic skills captured my personality.

Family and friends served as my test audience. They taught me how to better relate to the masses and instilled a shot of confidence at a critical time. Patti Baker is a dear and wise friend who is always there when called upon. Ann Saris donated many hours of her personal time along the way. Laura Regrine provided technical guidance early in the process. I have met so many other friends on this spiritual journey who have made life fun and exciting again…you all know who you are.

Finally, I need to thank my help from above. My Spirit Guides made me write this book and directed every step of the way. The Elders provided the wisdom that I think the world needs to hear. And God chose me as the servant to deliver his message. I am so humbled and honored to have been able to play this role!

RESOURCES AND RECOMMENDED READINGS

Intuitive Readers/Life Coaches

Holly Burns
hollyburnspsychic.com

Staci Wells
staciwells.com

Websites

Sacred Scribes, sacredscribes.blogspot.com, by Joanne Walmsley

The Jeshua Channelings, jeshua.net, by Pamela Kribbe and Garrit Gielen

Recommended Books

Living on Love: "The Messenger" by Klaus J. Joehle *(livingonlove.com)*

A Weekend With 'a' Drunken Leprechaun by Klaus J. Joehle

The Jeshua Channelings by Pamela Kribbe (jeshua.net)

Your Soul's Plan by Robert Schwartz

Whole by Brian Seth Hurst

The Power of Awareness by Neville

The Wisdom of Florence Scovel Shinn

Autobiography of a Yogi by Paramahansa Yogananda

The Power of Now by Eckhart Tolle

Follow us

Website: www.clearvessels.com

Email: steve@clearvessels.com

Instagram: @stevenjameshoffman

Facebook: www.facebook.com/stevenjameshoffman156

Get a free meditation: www.clearvessels.com/free-audio

About the Author

Steve grew up in South Dakota, a land that is as beautiful as it is demanding. Hard work and perseverance were the recipes for success for the generations who settled this land.

While these traits seemingly served Steve well, there came a point where he was forced to question this belief system. There must be more to life than working hard for someone else's definition of success. And where does God fit into all of this?

Through an opening caused by life's circumstances, Steve learned what a kind and compassionate Universe we live in. We are fully supported by a team of all-knowing Spirit Guides who like to have fun just as much as we do.

Steve has learned that joy, ease, and awareness are much more productive than "efforting" through life. He hopes his adult sons, Zach and Joe, can benefit from this knowledge in ways that Steve did not know about as they were growing up.

Residing in Wisconsin, Steve enjoys nature, college football, music festivals, and motorcycle riding.

Get a free meditation: www.clearvessels.com/free-audio

Made in the USA
Columbia, SC
24 October 2020